A New Retirement Blueprint

YOUR GUIDE TO A TAX EFFICIENT,
NON-CORRELATED AND HOLISTIC RETIREMENT

Allen Costellow

Southern Kentucky Advisors
BOWLING GREEN, KENTUCKY

Copyright © 2019 by Allen Costellow.

All rights reserved. No part of this publication may be reproduced, distributed or transmitted in any form or by any means, including photocopying, recording, or other electronic or mechanical methods, without the prior written permission of the publisher, except in the case of brief quotations embodied in critical reviews and certain other noncommercial uses permitted by copyright law.

Allen Costellow/Southern Kentucky Advisors
730 Fairview Ave., Suite B5
Bowling Green, KY 42101
https://sokyadvisors.com/

Information provided in this book is intended for educational purposes only and should not mistake as an offer to render personalized investment advice or financial planning advice.

Securities and Advisory Services offered through Client One Securities, LLC Member FINRA/SIPC and an Investment Advisor. Southern Kentucky Advisors, Inc. and Client One Securities, LLC are not affiliated.

Book Layout ©2015 BookDesignTemplates.com

New Retirement Blueprint / Allen Costellow. —2nd ed.

Contents

Foreword by Jim Britt i
Preface iii
Part One: Income Planning 1
    Part One: Action Items 25
Part Two: Investment Planning 27
    Part Two: Action Items 46
Part Three: Tax Planning 47
    Part Three: Action Items 61
Part Four: Health Care Planning 63
    Part Four: Action List 76
Part Five: Legacy Planning 77
    Part Five: Action List 83
Conclusion 85
Acknowledgments 87
About the Author 89
Contact Us 91

To my wife and the love of my life, Glenda.

As iron sharpens iron, so one man sharpens another

—Proverbs 27:17

Foreword
by Jim Britt

If you are like many who are preparing for retirement and wonder if your current advisor is the right person for getting you across the finish line, then this book may be the answer you have been looking for. The simple truth is that the methods you have used to accumulate your hard-earned funds are NOT the same methods required to make them last.

The one element that financially stable people of the world have in common is how easy it was for them to succeed financially when they finally understood how the money system worked and how to use it to their advantage.

The problem is this was never taught in high school, college or on the job. Up until now only the lucky few either had a family member or close friend share these wealth building insights, or they simply stumbled upon them by sheer trial and error. Not a good way to plan your financial future.

For over four decades Allen has been empowering retirees and their families with the knowledge necessary to thrive in their retirement years. The most amazing thing about gaining real financial security is how easy it is to attract once you know the rules of the game and play by those rules.

Can you just imagine the peace of mind you'll experience once you have a financial plan in place that can be measured and tested? This book truly delivers! You will get direct, action oriented financial building advice that works.

If you are not willing to act on the strategies Allen outlines in this content rich book, then my suggestion is don't buy it. If, however you are ready to learn to invest like the great endowments do for their patrons and could use a mentor with years of experience and a reputation for integrity, this book was written just for you.

You were born to be wealthy. Act now! You will probably want to keep this book near your elbow for quick reference, to read again and again on your way to financial peace of mind.

Jim Britt, 13-Time Best-Selling Author
www.jimbritt.com

Preface

The impact of the Baby Boomers generation has been like a tsunami. Many companies became household names and many industries experienced unprecedented growth as a result of this generation. Here are just a few: Gerber baby food, Olan Mills Photography, Wal-Mart, Fidelity Investments, and of course, the housing industry. As a group the boomers total almost 80 million people in the United States and over one billion worldwide.

Fittingly, as boomers exit the workforce, they continue to impact the United States retirement system. On January 1, 2008 the first boomer became eligible for Social Security. On January 1, 2011 the first boomer became eligible for Medicare. On July 2, 2016 the first boomer had to start taking their RMDs (required minimum distributions) from their qualified retirement plans. These dates will continue to impact the retirement system in the United States for the next thirty years, not only for the boomers but also for Generation Xers and Millennials. As a result, the planning models that many have accepted as gospel may need to be challenged and tested in ways previously not considered. It is no longer just a matter of rate of return and loss mitigation due to volatility. A significant increase in rate of return means little if the nest egg is depleted due to healthcare expenses wiping out what could have been passed to the next generation. And the next generation is going to need boomers to leave them something. As we will discuss, pension plans are becoming a thing of the past and Social Security benefits will likely have to be cut as well.

This is NOT your father's retirement. Today's retiree and their advisors must learn to think outside the box. Old ideas that have worked in the past may not meet the needs of today's retirees. Today's retirees must have a plan that is holistic and can be tracked and tested on a consistent basis. Those moving towards retirement must consider ALL five areas of concern if they are to survive and thrive in the future. Those five areas are income planning, investment planning, tax planning, healthcare planning, and legacy planning.

This book will take a deep dive into the issues and concerns facing retirees today. We will look at the history behind the current retirement system and discuss ways to improve the likelihood of success in the face of the changes that have happened and the challenges of dealing with these changes. Our focus will be on the five essential areas outlined above. Without a plan that includes all these areas and how each affects the other, many retirees find themselves looking for solutions from advisors who are still telling clients the same things they were 20 years ago!

Over the past 20 years one of the most successful approaches to earning consistent earnings, with lower volatility and exciting returns has been referred to by many as the "Endowment Model". This approach to investing has helped some of the major endowments such as Princeton and Yale achieve what is perhaps the best track record so far this millennium. So, what is it about the endowment model that makes it so special and how can it be applied to your retirement plans? Candidly, an endowment is not subject to the restraints that an individual is when it comes to their time line and as a result, the endowment model as practiced by the major endowments requires some modification when applied to individuals. For this reason, I have attempted to mirror our "New Retirement Blueprint" against many of the successful traits used in the endowment model, including allocations to private equity, real estate, and other alternative investments. Further, the Retirement Blueprint is careful to assure the retiree that ALL five areas of retirement are planned for. This holistic approach allows the retiree, or soon to be retiree, the opportunity to position funds (above and beyond what is required to generate sufficient cash flow) between principal protected and market assets in a way that allows them to sleep better knowing what their actual risk is. Further, by using alternative investments such as real estate, private equity and other income producing alternatives, a smaller amount of assets may be required to achieve the monthly income desired vs. the usual stock and bond mix touted by much of the industry. While many of these alternative investments may offer limited or no liquidity, the premium they pay for this inconvenience may exceed the problems illiquidity and additional risk may cause when used with care and while maintaining sufficient liquidity in other asset classes.

The combination of using multiple asset classes beyond the usual equity and debt products, combined with diversity within the asset classes may allow the retiree to achieve a balance between principal protection and growth, while providing the possibility for above-average income. This, coupled with a holistic approach to planning provides benefits that go beyond what many retirees are being offered.

Join me as we explore a whole new world of opportunity and look back through history at many of the decisions that brought us to the place, we find ourselves today.

PART ONE

Income Planning

"Your dad stays where he is because he understands he's building his three-legged stool: Social Security, personal savings, and his pension."

-Robert Woodward (My Grandfather)

Of the five areas covered in this book, (and in any retirement plan), the likelihood of success hinges on having enough income. The concepts put forward in the "Retirement Blueprint" hinge on the creation of sufficient income as the most important step to retirement success. For several decades this need was met by a concept known as the "three-legged stool of retirement." This "stool" was originally built on the premise that a social insurance program, coupled with private pensions and personal savings, could potentially eliminate the poverty that afflicted much of the nation's elderly during the Great Depression. Over the course of the past eighty years, many reactions to government legislation regarding the taxation of Social Security reshaped the landscape for today's retirees. This made things more important than ever for a retiree to have an integrated and holistic financial plan in place, versus a piecemeal approach. With the passage of time, we have moved from the original "three-legged stool" to one that in most cases only has two legs but, in nearly every case, one or more of the original legs is now shorter than was expected. These issues have created a potential crisis for 75 million baby boomers who have begun to receive the benefits they have contributed to for the past forty years. In this chapter we will explore how each leg of the three-legged stool has been shortened and offer ideas to increase the likelihood of success.

The year was 1961 when my dad took what would become his lifelong position making electric motors for a Fortune-500 company in a small town in south central Kentucky. As a young man of twenty-four with his whole life ahead of him and a first child on the way, I'm quite certain he did not expect that it would be almost forty years before he would leave this job.

When I was almost two years old, my mother was notified at her workplace that she needed to come to the local hospital as soon as possible to be with her husband who had just lost his arm in a die cast machine. Our lives would forever be impacted by the events of this day. Miraculously, my father survived the accident, even though it took the maintenance team over thirty minutes to get his arm removed from the machine. After a few days in the hospital and the amputation of what was left of his left arm, dad went home to convalesce. In six weeks, he was back on the job, and while he could no longer work in the die cast area of the plant, he was offered a position as a welder repairing the motors with minor defects that came off the assembly line.

His position with the company provided minimal opportunity for career advancement, but they did promise him that he "would always have a job." So, for thirty-eight years they kept their promise and he kept his. As our family grew and my only sibling was born, it always seemed that we had more month than money. I dreamed that one day my dad would get another job that paid more, and we could own our own home instead of moving from rental home to rental home. Don't misunderstand what I am saying, I never felt that I was a victim, and I am very grateful that no matter what happened, he provided for our needs, even if he couldn't provide for all our wants.

Before I was old enough to start working at odd jobs in the neighborhood, I found a way to contribute some funds to the family. I gathered and sold empty cola bottles. If you're under fifty and reading this, you probably have no idea what I'm talking about; it was a growing trend at this time to collect and resell bottles. This was my first entrepreneurial endeavor. I spent many hours searching for discarded bottles and got to know my local grocery store owner (who bought the bottles from me) well.

So, what does any of this have to do with income planning in retirement? I'm glad you asked. I could never understand why my dad stayed with the job he had, but when I was about ten years old, my grandfather explained a concept to me that I had never known before. He referred to it as the "three-legged stool." You see, in 1971 my grandfather was in his early seventies and still working as a sharecropper on the farm where he lived. I had asked him why dad continued to work at a job where I felt he didn't make enough money. He explained by using himself as an example.

My grandfather was born in 1900 and had spent his whole life working in agriculture, and other than Social Security he had no retirement income. He had never worked "public work" like my dad, and therefore did not qualify for a "pension," but he explained that my dad would receive a pension when he got to retirement age so that he would not have to keep working his whole life. For the first time in my life, I understood that my dad kept his job for several reasons, and the most important was to provide for me and my sister, but he also understood that while he was busy earning a weekly paycheck, his employer was putting money away to eventually provide a lifetime income for his later years. As of this writing, Dad is eighty-two and has been drawing his pension for twenty years.

As an adult I joined the financial services industry and began to further explore this idea of a "three-legged stool." According to my grandpa, President Roosevelt had shared this idea following the Great Depression. Historically speaking, Grandpa was correct about the concept, but not about who coined the term.

The Three-Legged Stool

With the kind of audience and following President Roosevelt commanded as the leader of the United States, it's not hard to imagine that many might think he came up with the metaphor of "the three-legged stool." A great orator, Roosevelt delivered about thirty or so radio addresses, or "fireside chats," during his presidency on topics from the banking crisis to unemployment to World War II efforts. He came up with many memorable phrases, such as "the only thing we have to fear is fear itself" and "when you come to the end of your rope, tie a knot and hang on." But I found in researching the history of the program that neither Roosevelt nor those who created the Social Security program in the mid-1930s coined the "three-legged stool" phrase. That credit goes to an insurance salesman.

According to an archival document on the Social Security Administration (ssa.gov) website, Reinhard A. Hohaus, an actuary for Metropolitan Life Insurance Company, is credited with using the term in a speech he gave at the Ohio Chamber of Commerce. In that 1949 speech, however, Hohaus described the three legs as consisting of private insurance, group insurance, and Social Security. Remember earlier, I mentioned many consider private pensions, personal savings, and Social Security to be the three legs.[1]

---

[1] Social Security Administration. 2019. "Agency History."
https://www.ssa.gov/history/stool.html.

The three-legged stool made sense as a good metaphor for depicting stability. After all, a stool requires a minimum of three legs to be able to sustain a person. You want your retirement money to be divvied up proportionally to take on the weight of you no longer working.

Roosevelt was elected in 1932. America and its citizens were desperate for some economic stability amidst the devastating effects of the Great Depression. People were suffering.

Creating Social Security

During his first inaugural address in 1933, Roosevelt announced that "... the only thing we have to fear is fear itself."

Roosevelt moved quickly to implement changes that would forever shape the face of the American economy and the American political process. Banks were still in a crisis and they were the topic of his very first fireside chat, given within two months of him taking office.

Beginning with his New Deal, Roosevelt swiftly addressed many key issues, including the establishment of the FDIC and the Glass Stegall Act. The first provided government guarantees of bank deposits and the second created a wall between Main Street and Wall Street that would remain in effect for over fifty years. But the most significant and lasting legislation came in his New Deal Two: the establishment of what would become the Social Security Administration.

In June 1934, Roosevelt announced that his administration would develop a social insurance program. It wasn't a uniquely American innovation. According to the SSA website, by the time Roosevelt signed the Social Security Act on the afternoon of August 14, 1935, some thirty-four nations already had some type of social insurance program.

Initially, the Social Security Act was an unfunded mandate. The independent Social Security Board created by the act didn't have a budget. Its first budget was pulled from the funds of the Federal Emergency Relief Administration, the agency that would be replaced by another well-known Roosevelt initiative, the Works Progress Administration or WPA. Its staff and even furniture for its offices were cobbled together from other agencies.

Can you imagine the work it took to get that initial system pulled together—of assigning Social Security numbers, establishing work histories, calculating benefits, and more? The U.S. Postal Service was contracted to help distribute initial applications and assign numbers. SSA history says the first cards and numbers were issued sometime in mid-November 1936. On December 1, 1936, the Social Security headquarters office in Baltimore, Maryland, got a stack of the first 1,000 records. The first record pulled from that stack belonged to twenty-three-year-old John D. Sweeney of New Rochelle, New York, who was working as a shipping clerk in the family business. Sweeney died at age sixty-one, never personally receiving any benefits.

The first person to receive a Social Security "old-age" benefit was retired legal secretary Ida M. Fuller, sixty-five, who was issued a check on January 31, 1940 for $22.54—just $2.21 shy of what she'd paid in on three years of work (between Social Security being established in 1936 and when she retired in 1939). Living until the age of one hundred, Fuller would eventually collect $22,888.92 in total.

The Social Security Board eventually lost its independent status in 1939 and was renamed the Social Security Administration in 1946. It was shuffled to other government agencies until President Clinton made it an independent agency again in 1995.

So, what was so special about the age of sixty-five to make it a marker for when to start paying out benefits? Germany, one of the early adopters of a social insurance program, was using sixty-five, but that wasn't the prevailing reason America went with it. The government committee that came up with the eventual Social Security program looked at the retirement ages being used in the approximate thirty state-level pension plans in the U.S.—about half used sixty-five and the remainder used seventy—and the retirement age of sixty-five was used in the 1934 federal Railroad Retirement System.

Out of Proportion

The idea of creating a social safety net to provide a minimal amount of income in retirement was a critical idea promoted by the New Deal president. I am not sure Mr. Roosevelt, the actuaries who originally designed Social Security, or the people for whom it was created could have ever imagined what the program was destined to become.

Social Security wasn't meant to be *the* primary leg in that "three-legged stool" metaphor. But that's what happened in the more than eight decades since it was created. The Social Security Administration says Social Security is the major source of income for most of the elderly. According to its 2018 fact sheet, "Among elderly Social Security beneficiaries, 48 percent of married couples and 69 percent of unmarried persons receive 50 percent or more of their income from Social Security." More than 60 percent of elderly beneficiaries (21 percent of married couples and about 44 percent of unmarried persons) rely on Social Security for 90 percent or more of their income.[2] It's just not practical or realistic for a stool to have one of its legs so significantly out of proportion. The original intent of the Social Security program was to be one of three legs in the retirement income stool, but many today are

---

[2] Social Security Administration. 2018. "Fact Sheet; Social Security." https://www.ssa.gov/news/press/factsheets/basicfact-alt.pdf

struggling or even unable to sustain the other two legs. That's leaving them in the same precarious economic conditions that the system had hoped to rectify when it was started.

Remember the other legs of the stool—pensions and personal savings? According to that SSA 2018 fact sheet, "50 percent of the workforce in private industry have no private pension coverage," and "36 percent of workers report they and/or their spouse have not personally saved any money for retirement."[3] With many forces at work—from employers looking to cut costs and Americans eager to consume—we've forgotten about the formula that would help keep that stool balanced.

Lifting above Poverty

Social Security plays a significant economic role in America today. Not only is Social Security being relied upon heavily by the elderly and retired workers, but it is also a major factor in keeping dependents and other adults out of poverty. According to the Center on Budget and Policy Priorities and data from the Census Bureau's March 2018 Current Population Survey, more than 22 million Americans—including 5.6 million adults under age sixty-four and 1.1 million children—are kept above the poverty line by Social Security benefits. (Before the first retirement check was even issued to retired worker Ida M. Fuller in 1940, the Social Security Act was amended to include survivors and dependents of deceased workers.)

For more than 39 million elderly Americans today, if they didn't collect Social Security, they'd fall below the poverty line. Other vulnerable groups that are kept out of poverty by Social Security are women and people of color. Inconsistencies in pay, life

---

[3] Ibid.

expectancies, and disabilities are all pressures that occur in nearly all working groups outside of white men.

Social Security: High Stakes

After more than eighty years since its formation and with so many demographic changes in the U.S.—the large baby boomer population pushing into retirement, longer life expectancies and fewer births—Social Security will have a hard time existing into its second century.

According to 2018 government reports, in its lifetime Social Security has collected about $20.9 trillion in taxes and interest and has paid out $18 trillion in benefits. Do the math and you know that has left $2.9 trillion. With fewer people in the workforce to continue paying in and sustain the coffers and baby boomers and the generation before them living longer, those reserves will be whittled away by the year 2034. That's one hundred years after Roosevelt announced his administration would form a social insurance program.

Know the Rules

Understanding the rules and regulations of the Social Security program are of critical importance in planning for retirement. Making the wrong choice can cost hundreds of thousands of dollars in lost benefits. Instead, you want to maximize all your financial retirement options.

For example, because of several changes made to the program over the years, the SSA became aware of "unintended loopholes" that created some strategies that were being used primarily by married couples to maximize retirement benefits. In the Bipartisan Budget Act of 2015, Congress closed two of those loopholes.

One of them, for example, had allowed a retired worker—usually the higher earner—to file to open benefits and then suspend their own collection of those benefits. However, the spouse could then start collecting on the benefit while the worker then earned credit for delaying collection. (By suspending and foregoing collection until later years, the worker would earn DRCs or delayed retirement credit and build up a beefier fund in the interim.) Now, if a worker's record is filed and suspended, no one can collect on the benefit.

Peculiarities such as this closed loophole and others make having professional help mandatory if you are to navigate the waters that we find ourselves in.

For example, it's pretty common knowledge that most retirees claim their Social Security as soon as they turn age sixty-two.[4] Further, past logic taught that one should forgo using qualified funds as long as possible. For many retirees today, the opposite is mathematically more correct. Delaying Social Security benefits past full retirement age (FRA) allows benefits to grow by 8 percent per year until age seventy. Since few retirement accounts earn a guaranteed 8 percent growth, it may make more sense to go ahead and spend qualified funds and allow Social Security benefits to grow unless the beneficiary is in poor health or has a short family life expectancy. The key to this and most decisions about retirement is to make a math decision versus an emotional decision.

If you feel like your three-legged stool is a little shorter than you expected, one cause for this is the taxation of Social Security.

Social Security taxation is a subject that we will address further in part three, but once a retiree reaches full retirement age (FRA), a beneficiary can earn as much money as they want without having

---

[4] Dan Caplinger. The Motley Fool. June 19, 2018. "What's the Most Popular Age to Take Social Security? A Foolish Take."
https://www.usatoday.com/story/money/personalfinance/retirement/2018/06/19/whats-most-popular-age-to-take-social-security/35928543/

to give Social Security benefits back. That was until the onset of "Provisional Income Taxation" was implemented. Keep reading to learn more.

Today's retiree will generally have greater resources than those prior to Roosevelt's New Deal(s), but they will also be faced with new issues that have created a financial landscape that can be treacherous and unforgiving. Making the wrong decision about Social Security claiming strategies can be devastating. My vision and passion are to help retirees make the right decisions at the right time, so they can live their life on their terms.

Pensions and 401(k) Plans

Pensions and 401(k) plans are types of retirement plans that are tied to one's employment. A pension, however, is considered a defined-benefit plan where the employer pays in money to the plan and then pays out a specified amount (usually set through a union or other contract), while a 401(k) plan is a defined contribution plan that requires you to contribute to the plan while your employer may provide additional amounts.

Pensions have a much longer history but seem to be falling out of favor for reasons that include the declining influence of labor unions and being costlier for employers.

According to an October 2018 report from the Bureau of Labor Statistics, only 4 percent of all private industry workers have access to a defined benefit plan, while 51 percent have access to a defined contribution plan. Thirteen percent have access to both.[5]

---

[5] Bureau of Labor Statistics. October 2, 2019. "51 Percent of Private Industry Workers had Access to Only Defined Contribution Retirement Plans."
https://www.bls.gov/opub/ted/2018/51-percent-of-private-industry-workers-had-access-to-only-defined-contribution-retirement-plans-march-2018.htm

History of the U.S. Pension

Borrowing from the British, the Continental Congress in 1755 set up a pension program for the soldiers it enlisted to fight in the American Revolution. But it would take a century before the first private sector pension plan was created, when The American Express Company started offering its employees such a plan in 1875.

Prior to the 1870s, private sector plans did not exist. Most companies up to this point were small mom-and-pop businesses and funding a pension would have been an undertaking beyond the scope of that day and time.

With the industrialization of the American worker, the rise of large companies such as Standard Oil, U.S. Steel, General Electric, and AT&T, along with workers demanding fair and equitable treatment, the pension became a staple of the American worker. By 1929 there were 329 employer pension plans in the United States and Canada.

One of the primary reasons for the expansion of pensions in America was the Revenue Act of 1921. This act exempted interest income for stock bonus or profit-sharing plans from current taxation. Trust income was taxed as it was distributed to employees only to the extent that it exceeded employee's own contributions. With this change in the tax code, the door was opened for an expansion of this new idea. In 1926 the Revenue Act was expanded to exempt income of pension trusts from current taxation, and in 1928 employers could take tax deductions for reasonable amounts paid into the pension trust required to fund current liabilities. From this point forward until the passage of ERISA in 1974 a pension was considered a part of an employee benefit package. Most people stayed with one employer for most of their life (remember my dad) and the benefit of a promised pension was a primary reason for this loyalty. In 1938, a revenue ruling known as the "nondiversion" rule made pension trusts irrevocable, and by 1940 over

4.1 million private sector workers (15 percent of the private-sector workforce) were covered by a pension plan.

Following the Revenue Act of 1940, there was a plethora of new laws affecting just about every aspect of the American financial system and many of those carried over to pensions as well. One example is the Investment Advisor Act of 1940. After passage of this law, pension funds were required to be managed by an investment advisor. Between 1940 and 1980, more than two dozen additional laws and/or rulings were passed that affected pensions, including the establishment of the Pension Benefit Guaranty Association (PBGA) in 1974. By the time of passage of PBGA, private-sector pensions had reached their highest level—46 percent of all workers.

The Decline of Pensions

Numerous reports and economic experts have cited the steady decline of defined plans or pensions being offered by employers. Depending on the defined-plan agreement between an employer and its employees, a pension can be considered an effective retirement plan since some plans can pay a monthly amount equivalent to 50 percent of what the worker earned while employed.

But on the flip side, for employers, a defined plan often has higher costs. If, for example, future benefit obligations for an employer go up because of salary increases or the hiring of a higher-paid employee–the liabilities and cost of the plan go up for the employer.

The decline of labor unions has also led to a decline in workers having access to pension plans. Labor unions have been strong advocates of pension plans. But the number of American workers who belong to labor unions has declined from the union's peak point in the mid-1950s when more than 30 percent of workers were members to just 11 percent in mid-2018, according to *The Economist*. In the private sector, only 7 percent of workers belong to unions.[6]

This exodus away from the defined-benefit retirement plans (a.k.a. pensions) is causing an income crisis and has many people wondering how they will be able to pay for their seemingly ever-increasing cost of living as they age. Original pension plans offered key factors that assured their success including but not limited to:

1. Professional management
2. Long-term investment horizon
3. Actuarial arbitrage
4. Access to alternative investments

A typical retiree who is forced to provide a pension-like income from personal investing is put at a significant disadvantage that most are not prepared to handle. The financial services industry is built more for the accumulation of wealth than the preservation and providing of guaranteed lifetime income. Guaranteed lifetime income has historically been the arena of the insurance section of the financial services industry.

Pensions consider longevity among large numbers of people (much like an insurance company) into their calculation of benefits. In fact, many pension plans contract with insurance companies to provide the lifetime benefits promised to their employees when the time comes to begin withdrawals. In the past, the worker had very few options about this process. My father receives exactly the same amount per month from his pension today that he started drawing from almost twenty years ago, and the monthly

---

[6] The Economist. July 19th, 2018. "How the Decline of Unions will Change America." https://www.economist.com/united-states/2018/07/19/how-the-decline-of-unions-will-change-america

check comes from an insurance company. Most pension benefits are provided by annuity payments from insurance companies; this has always been an area where the insurance sector of the financial services industry has played an important role.

In 1979 a British new wave rock group called "The Buggles" had a number one hit in the United States called "Video Killed the Radio Star." In 1981, this same tune became the first music video ever shown on MTV. I share this story because of the interesting timeline between the song's release and the subsequent release of the video and the creation of the modern day 401(k) plan which would begin the demise of the employer pension plan.

The Start of the 401(k) Plan

The 401(k) plan gets its name from a section of the Internal Revenue Code that Ted Benna realized could be creatively interpreted to create a tax-deferred, defined-contribution payment plan. Benna was a retirement benefit consultant and co-owner with the Pennsylvania-based firm, The Johnson Cos.

The section had been revised in 1978 for another reason, but Benna realized it could have applications as a tax-deferred, profit-sharing plan, the kind one of his clients was looking for to offer to its employees in lieu of a cash bonus plan. At the time Benna was studying the section, defined-contribution plans existed but they did not have the tax-deferred element. While the client ended up rejecting the plan based on fears it might be appealed, Benna and his company started offering the plan in 1981.

Today's financial service industry has profited highly from Ted's creation. For the first time in United States history, employers could deduct funds for retirement on a tax-deferred basis and offer a match from the employer and defer taxes on gains to a time in the future. Wall Street quickly saw the potential for profit, and while investing in individual stocks would not be conducive to the design of the 401(k) plan, the mutual fund was a perfect fit. In 1979 there was approximately $40 billion invested in United States mutual funds. In 2017 that number was in excess of $17 trillion with almost $6 trillion being held in 401(k) plans.[7]

When reviewing one's financial continuum, there are three distinct phases: accumulation, preservation, and distribution. Most mutual funds were specifically designed for the accumulation of wealth, and they have done an amazing job of helping the average person to accumulate tremendous amounts of wealth systematically. It is quite possible that this wealth would not have been accumulated without the mutual fund as a vehicle.

The second phase of one's financial life is preservation, and while there are funds specifically designed for income (such as bond funds), there is still the potential for loss of principal and no guarantee of lifetime income. The problem in the financial world we live in is that many advisors are telling clients that mutual funds can do the job of a true income product such as annuities. I am not very mechanically inclined, but even I know that the chance of success is greatly improved when you use the right tools. Trying to create guaranteed lifetime income with a product designed for long-term growth doesn't make a lot of sense. It would be like using a race car for a tractor. Sounds silly, but this is the logic many people are being expected to follow.

As an advisor, my role is not to implement my personal values on my clients, but rather to help them choose financial products that mirror their personal values and financial needs. Many retirees come to me without any sort of private or governmental pension to provide basic needs on a guaranteed basis but have been told by their current advisor that they can continue to follow the advice that got them to retirement, *for* retirement.

---

[7] New York Times, Aug. 24, 1979. ICI Factbook. https://www.icifactbook.org/

They just need to reduce withdrawal rates to somewhere between 2.7 and 4.0 percent. This percentage has changed several times over the past decade, but on January 21, 2013, Morningstar published a report titled "Low Bond Yields and Safe Portfolio Withdrawal Rates" that used the Nobel Prize-winning Modern Portfolio Theory strategy of a stock and bond mix to generate "safe" withdrawal rates. As you can see from the following chart, a withdrawal rate of 2.8 percent is used for the standard 60/40 equity/bond mix and 2.7 percent for an 80/20 mix.

LOW BOND YIELDS AND SAFE PORTFOLIO WITHDRAWAL RATES
JANUARY 21, 2013

REMEMBER MORNINGSTAR
RETIREMENT PERIOD (YEARS)

Is this what being a millionaire in America has become?

PROBABILITY OF SUCCESS	20% EQUITY ALLOCATION						40% EQUITY ALLOCATION					
	15	20	25	30	35	40	15	20	25	30	35	40
99	5.0	3.6	2.8	2.2	1.9	1.6	4.6	3.3	2.5	2.1	1.8	1.6
95	5.4	4.0	3.1	2.6	2.2	1.9	5.2	3.9	3.1	2.6	2.2	2.0
90	5.7	4.2	3.3	2.7	2.3	2.1	5.6	4.2	3.4	2.8	2.5	2.2
80	6.0	4.4	3.5	3.0	2.6	2.3	6.1	4.6	3.7	3.2	2.8	2.5
50	6.6	5.0	4.1	3.4	3.0	2.7	7.0	5.5	4.5	3.9	3.5	3.2

PROBABILITY OF SUCCESS	60% EQUITY ALLOCATION						80% EQUITY ALLOCATION					
99	3.9	2.8	2.2	1.9	1.5	1.3	3.4	2.3	1.8	1.4	1.2	1.1
95	4.9	3.6	2.8	2.4	2.0	1.8	4.4	3.2	2.6	2.1	1.8	1.6
90	5.4	4.0	3.2	2.7	2.4	2.2	5.1	3.8	3.0	2.6	2.2	2.0
80	6.1	4.6	3.8	3.2	2.9	2.6	5.8	4.6	3.7	3.2	2.8	2.6
50	7.4	5.9	4.9	4.3	3.9	3.6	7.8	6.2	5.3	4.6	4.2	3.9

$1,000,000 @2.7% = $27,000 before taxes!

These are the **safe** withdrawal rates.

Source: https://corporatemorningstar.com/us/documents/targetmaturity/LowBondYieldsWithdrawalRAtes.pdf

The MOST important thing to remember from the preceding chart is that the withdrawal rates shown are NOT suggesting that you will leave anything behind, but rather the rates of withdrawal (which includes the possible use of principal) should get you to the end of life.

Let's put this into actual dollar amounts and see what that looks like. If you have one million dollars saved today in your 401(k) or IRA, then current logic suggests that you live on $27,000 per year (before taxes) in order to keep you in their version of a financial plan. Wow, I never thought being a millionaire would only allow me to spend $27,000 per year. Did you? After all, the stock market averages over 12 percent per year, right? That's what we have been told by all the radio pundits for the past twenty-plus years. So, if it's true that the market averages 12 percent per year, why can't we count on living on 12 percent per year? The answer is found in the creative math used by Wall Street and many advisors. Average returns work well in the accumulation phase of your financial life, but they may destroy your chances of success during the withdrawal phase of your life. Check out the following charts.

Beginning retirement asset value = $1,000,000
Number of years = 30

10% of beginning value = ($100,000)
Average return = 14.84%

CONSTANT RETURNS

RETIREMENT YEAR	ANNUAL RETURN	ANNUAL INCOME	ACCOUNT VALUE
1	14.84%	-$100,000	$1,033,290
2	14.84%	-$100,000	$1,072,100
3	14.84%	-$100,000	$1,116,360
4	14.84%	-$100,000	$1,167,188
5	14.84%	-$100,000	$1,225,558
6	14.84%	-$100,000	$1,292,591
7	14.84%	-$100,000	$1,369,572
8	14.84%	-$100,000	$1,457,976
9	14.84%	-$100,000	$1,559,500
10	14.84%	-$100,000	$1,676,090
11	14.84%	-$100,000	$1,809,982
12	14.84%	-$100,000	$1,963,743
13	14.84%	-$100,000	$2,140,322
14	14.84%	-$100,000	$2,343,106
15	14.84%	-$100,000	$2,575,983
20	14.84%	-$100,000	$4,373,434
25	14.84%	-$100,000	$7,963,668
30	14.84%	-$100,000	$15,134,818

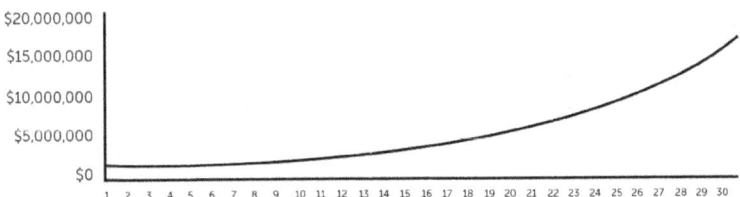

As you can see from the preceding chart, if your one million dollars earned the *average* return of 14.84 percent (the average of the S&P 500 from 1970 to 1999) on a constant basis, you could pull $100,000 per year from the account and at the end of thirty years have over $15,000,000 left in your estate! Wow sign me up! But the truth is, the market does not earn constant returns. In fact, they are anything but constant. Let's look at what happens when we take out the same $100,000 from the same one-million-dollar account but receive average returns of 14.84 percent, but not constant returns of 14.84 percent.[8]

Beginning retirement asset value = $1,000,000
Number of years = 30

10% of beginning value = ($100,000)
Average return = 14.84%

FLUCTUATING RETURNS

YEAR	ANNUAL RETURN	ANNUAL INCOME	ACCOUNT VALUE
1	3.99%	-$100,000	$935,910
2	14.33%	-$100,000	$955,696
3	18.94%	-$100,000	$1,017,765
4	-14.79%	-$100,000	$782,027
5	-26.54%	-$100,000	$501,017
6	37.25%	-$100,000	$550,396
7	23.67%	-$100,000	$557,005
8	-7.39%	-$100,000	$423,232
9	6.44%	-$100,000	$344,048
10	18.35%	-$100,000	$288,831
11	32.27%	-$100,000	$249,767
12	-5.05%	-$100,000	$142,204
13	21.48%	-$100,000	$51,269
14	22.50%	$-51,269	$0
15	6.15%	$0	$0

This chart presents the answer to why Morningstar says a withdrawal rate of 2.7 percent is what you should live on in order to not run out of money. Perhaps the biggest risk investors face in retirement is sequence of returns risk. Investors who have both Social Security and a pension may be better able to stay the course when markets are volatile, but those needing consistent income may want to investigate other ways of generating cash flow that are not tied to sequence of returns risk.

---

[8] Morningstar. January 2013. Low Bond Yields and Safe Portfolio Withdrawal Rates.

As of the date of this writing, the stock market just finished one of the worst fourth quarters since the Great Depression after having an amazing first, second, and third quarter. If you were retiring in January of 2019, you would most likely be doing so with 10 to 20 percent less in your account than you had in September 2018 when it looked like the market would never go down. Does this mean you should jump ship and move all your funds to the safety of an FDIC-insured account and just suffer the loss you have endured? Unfortunately, this is exactly what many retirees will be doing in the coming months. Taking this action may be as destructive as the losses of the fourth quarter of 2018. In the coming sections we will examine various investment strategies, but for our purposes in this section it is paramount that those who do not have the benefit of a pension consider acting to secure a portion of their funds to provide a constant cash flow and preferably one that they cannot outlive.

Over the past twenty years, the growth of a new form of insurance product called fixed indexed annuities has enjoyed unprecedented growth among retirees as a safe haven for accumulated wealth or to provide guaranteed lifetime income like what a pension offers.[9]

I am a true believer in capitalism. I have observed throughout my career that the capitalistic market will usually deliver what the consumer is looking for, and this is the case with the growth in fixed indexed annuities. For your free white paper report on the benefits, costs and fees associated with this option go to www.sokyadvisors.com and request a free copy of "The ABCs of FIAs."

---

[9] Guarantees are backed by the financial strength and claims-paying ability of the issuing insurance company.

Personal Savings

The third and final leg of the retirement stool was to be personal savings. The idea of a "nest egg" that was to be protected and nurtured is as old as humanity. In ancient times and today in third-world nations, one's children were considered the "nest egg" for the elderly, but that concept has been pretty much lost in today's modern world. Hillary Clinton once stated that "it takes a village" to raise a child. I was one of those children who can relate to needing a village. Without the help of aunts, uncles, and especially grandparents, my childhood could have been tough. But thanks to a loving and close-knit extended family, I grew up without ever realizing that things were difficult for us. When I was nine years old, my grandmother became very sick with diabetes and subsequently lost both legs. Since a nursing home was not a consideration, my aunts and uncles (all seven of them) took a night and stayed with my grandparents and took care of the matriarch of our family. My grandparents were teenagers during World War One and were building a family throughout the Great Depression and World War Two. They believed that hard work, staying out of debt, and not giving up was the formula for success. I am thankful for the heritage they gave me.

It was assumed that ongoing saving on a personal level would be continued after the birth of Social Security. The mindset of the generation when it was introduced in 1935 would have been that whatever they had it would be dependent on their own savings. With shorter life expectancies at that time, most people considered that they would just keep working if they couldn't meet their needs through saving. According to the Social Security Administration's online history pages, the Great Depression had pushed a lot of elderly into poverty, with many losing their jobs and livelihoods. Roosevelt wanted to provide stability for America's economy and its citizens. I believe he was correct in wanting to provide that stability, but many things changed over the years.

The idea of retirement was a fairly new one, because prior to Social Security, the elderly continued working until they could not work anymore. Roosevelt wanted to preserve the dignity of the elderly and his belief was that a people who already understood the requirement to save, coupled with a new social insurance plus a probable pension would be enough to allow the elderly to retire with dignity. All three legs of the stool have been trimmed substantially by circumstances unforeseen at the genesis of his New Deal.

It is hard for those of us in the "baby boomer" generation to grasp the idea of losing funds safely tucked away in a bank. That is because of the many financial changes that were implemented following the Great Depression. It took several years for faith in the banking industry to be restored, but with the passage of the FDIC act, people began to bring their funds back to the banks. Today, money in a bank is considered the lowest risk one can take, and interest earned on savings is considered the foundational start of a lifelong financial plan.

The post-Great Depression survivors were savers. They knew what it meant to be under the thumb of a debtor, and many understood what it meant to be hungry. Taking a handout would not have been acceptable. For this reason, Social Security was designed that beneficiaries would contribute to the program and thus always be the recipient of funds they had helped to build.

Today's financial advice is not to save, but rather to maintain an emergency account because savings accounts pay so little. In fact, I just googled "best savings account rates" and found an "amazing" offer of 2.15 percent% for a five-year CD! According to the U.S. Inflation Rate website, the last twelve months since this writing saw up to 2.4 percent inflation.[10] So, if you were a saver, you just safely lost purchasing power over the past year.

The 2018 average savings rate in the United States is 7.6 percent.[11] This includes funds inside 401(k) accounts. The average person at age sixty today has less than $60,000 saved. For most families, that is barely enough to cover two years in retirement.

The traditional thought is, as we age, we are in a better position to add to our savings account—maybe because we've learned to handle our money more efficiently, or we've reduced certain debt (such as home mortgages). Hopefully, we're increasing our earnings too.

Using data from the Federal Reserve and the Federal Deposit Insurance Corporation, a study in mid-2018 looked at the savings statistics among three age groups. The median savings for millennials (born 1981 to 1998) was $2,430, for Generation X (born 1965 to 1980) it was $15,780, and for baby boomers and older (born before 1964) it was $24,280. That's hardly enough savings to have on hand for emergencies, much less retirement. [12]

At the time of the coining of the term "Three-Legged Stool," it was understood that personal savings were in fact savings, not investing. It was generally assumed that the future retiree would live off Social Security and their pension with their personal savings allocated to balance out financial needs when the first two did not meet that month's expenses. The savings component was to be protected and nourished, not exposed to loss.

---

[10] Trading Economics. 2019. United States Inflation Rate.
https://tradingeconomics.com/united-states/inflation-cpi
[11] Bureau of Economic Analysis. March 29, 2019. "Personal Saving Rate."
https://www.bea.gov/data/income-saving/personal-saving-rate
[12] Magnify Money. August 23, 2018. "How Much Does the Average American Have in Savings?"
https://www.magnifymoney.com/blog/news/average-american-savings/

Low interest rates and market volatility have made the idea of saving money very difficult for some people. Why save money at 2 percent when inflation is 2.7 percent? As a result, many are entering retirement with very small amounts of money in savings and thus the third leg of the three-legged stool has been affected, too.

For those reading this book under the age of sixty and still working, one place to consider putting saved dollars may be a high cash-value and low death-benefit life insurance plan offered by a mutual insurance company. This type of product not only provides the protection of a death benefit, but also has the potential for above-average growth through dividend payments from the insurance company's profits from operations. For more information on this strategy, go to www.sokyadvisors.com and request your free report, "The Four Buckets of Tax Planning".

Part One: Action Items

1. Check your future Social Security income amounts today. If you don't already have an account, go to www.ssa.gov and create your personal account today and check it regularly. When you meet with an advisor, be certain to bring a current report.
2. Attend a workshop on Social Security claiming strategies. You can register for an upcoming event with our company at www.sokyadvisors.com.
3. Develop a firm budget divided into three categories and determine how you hope to achieve each one, but making sure essential needs are planned for first.
   a. Essential
   b. Desired
   c. Wish list

4. Develop a comprehensive Income Plan that allows you to organize, track and most importantly *test* your potential outcomes. Doing an online Monte Carlo simulation is *not* enough. You will need a written plan that can be organized, tracked year after year, and tested in real time against potential changes. To schedule a consultation with an advisor from Southern Kentucky Advisors simply go to www.sokyadvisors.com and click on "schedule a consultation."

PART TWO

Investment Planning

"Don't worry. You're in it for the long haul."

-Your Current Investment Advisor

In 1999, I was president of a company I had started a few years before in partnership with a family-controlled mutual insurance company. We were marketing insurance and financial services to retirees in an eight-state area. We had grown the company from zero to more than 28,000 new clients in just over three years. On June 15, 1999, my partner and I decided to go our separate ways, mostly because we could no longer agree on the direction of the company's future growth.

A few weeks later, I was bought out and as part of the buyout, I agreed to honor a six-month no-compete clause, during which time I could not be employed in the financial services industry. I was thirty-eight years old, and it was a very interesting period in my life, as I had been gainfully employed since I was thirteen. This was the first time I had time on my hands and no need for a paycheck. It was like being involuntarily retired. I spent my days having lunch with friends, playing golf, spending time with my wife (who was expecting our fifth child), and reading. I have always been an avid reader, but during those six months I added (and read) more books to my personal library than any other period of my life. I read *Beating the Street* by Peter Lynch. I re-read *The Richest Man in Babylon* by George Clason. I read *Unlimited Power* by Tony Robbins. I then bought a small book called *Rich Dad, Poor Dad* by Robert Kiyosaki.

It was Kiyosaki's book that lead me to another book by the same author called *The Cashflow Quadrant*. It was from the second book that I began to formulate a plan for the work I do today. Reading these books made me realize I no longer wanted to be a salesperson of financial products, but rather build a company that equipped people for their retirement years. This undoubtedly meant financial products would be used, but not as stand-alone solutions. Instead, they would act as bricks and mortar in the construction of individualized plans.

The company I had sold in 1999 was built on selling products. The company I wanted to create would be built on planning. As happens so many times in life, my plan was put on hold for almost fifteen years. During this time, I built two other companies and became a Vice President for a Fortune-500 company, opening new financial service offices and training advisors. During my three years with the Fortune-500 company, we opened over thirty new offices and recruited and trained hundreds of new advisors across the country. A few years later, I was offered a chance to go back to work for the firm I had sold in 1999. We moved the company back to Bowling Green, Kentucky, where I had originally started in 1995. Over the next eighteen months, I opened eight new offices and trained over one hundred new advisors. Then, life happened.

I experienced a health scare that caused me to rethink every area of my life. It was at this time that I realized it was time to launch the vision I had many years before to build a company based on planning and not products. The lessons I learned from the books were many, but the one I want to share regarding investing is a statement made by Robert Kiyosaki. He says when he invests money, he does so for cash flow. If his investment goes up, that's good, but he wants cash flow along the way. This was quite different from what most of the financial services industry taught, but it made a lot of sense to me. If you have not read the book *Rich Dad, Poor Dad*, go and buy a copy. It's a short read, and it will open your eyes to ideas about investing that you may have never seen before.

As you are probably aware, most financial education, licensing, and registrations equip you to sell insurance and investments as either an employee of a large firm, or as a self-employed person in your own firm. I chose not to take the path of working as an employee for one of the big firms because I wanted what I felt was greater independence by being on my own with a small firm. However, I did not want to build a business that was totally dependent on me. I have spent most of my life building firms from the ground up through recruiting and training financial service representatives and building administrative systems. My vision was to build a firm that had the backing of a strong broker-dealer relationship and Registered Investment Advisor platform, but also did not restrict me from integrating outside products such as fixed indexed annuities, asset-based long-term care, life insurance, disability income, and other products and services required to build a holistic plan for my clients. I wanted the freedom to work with my clients on an individual and not a cookie-cutter approach. I was committed to this vision even if it meant starting my own broker-dealer and/or Registered Investment Advisor firm.

Fortunately, I now work with a medium sized firm in Kansas that allows me the freedom I was looking for without having to start from scratch. This relationship continues to grow and will prosper over time and will allow me to not only add new clients personally, but to grow our firm through mentoring and training other advisors who share my vision of a holistic approach to financial planning. Over the years my philosophy of investing has grown and matured as I have had the opportunity to be mentored by many successful people in our industry. One of my mentors helped to inspire my vision and intention behind the ideas outlined in the New Retirement Blueprint approach to planning.Let me share my investing philosophy.

Investing is about individual philosophy, and mine can be spelled out as simply as: I-S-G.

I = Income.

S = Safety.

G = Growth.

As you have learned from Part One of this book, income planning is truly the cornerstone of a solid financial plan. In our last section, however, we did not take a deep dive into *how* to generate income in retirement when a retiree does not have a pension to fall back on. While we will cover all three parts of the I-S-G formula for successful retirement planning in this portion of the book, we will begin with how to allocate investments to produce income. These ideas can be used to generate lifestyle income, take the place of a non-existent pension, or simply provide tax-free income if you have enough time to maximize the use of whole life insurance.

I = Income

When CD rates hit 15.33 percent, I was only twenty years old. My financial plan was to put enough money into the "bank" to create a $50,000 per year income. All I needed was to save $333,000! By the time I was anywhere close to having saved this amount of money, inflation had cut the purchase power of $50,000 to $32,258 and interest on $333,000 would only generate $13,986. Thank goodness I learned this lesson early in life! This example clearly shows how difficult it is to "plan" for income. Between the twin demons of inflation and fluctuating interest rates, the old days of income planning based on the safety of bank rates, or for that matter, the rates offered by bonds, has become antiquated. As we discussed in the previous section of this book, historical interest rates are not properly reflected by the excessive rates of the 1980s, nor the incredibly low rates of the past decade, but rather they are expressed on a large-scale level by the inflation we experience as a country.

As you may recall from section one, a 2013 report by Morningstar suggests, with a typical 60/40 (stock/bond) split, that a 2.8 percent withdrawal rate was considered "safe."[13] And as we previously discussed, if you had a million dollars in retirement assets, with $400,000 in equities and $600,000 in bonds, you would need to live on approximately $27,000 per year in order to remain safe. Income is the end result of all investing, but when income is needed, it should play heavily into the choices made about the underlying investment approach. Let's look at three different potential income scenarios.

Scenario One: Income Now

How can we generate "income now?" It depends on when "now" is. There are several strategies for generating income that are beyond the scope of the 60/40 split. The 60/40 split was a great solution for many years, but times have changed. It's important that your advisor and the firm he or she represents is willing and able to do more than the status quo. Many professionals are working with their hands tied and are not allowed to offer products that may very well meet the needs of today's income-hungry investor.

---

[13] David Blanchett, Michael Finke, Wade D. Pfau. Morningstar. January 21, 2013. "Low Bond Yields and Safe Portfolio Withdrawal Rates."
http://static.fmgsuite.com/media/documents/c6736c14-ae86-45d3-8edb-e30746317603.pdf

For this reason, working with an independent advisor who can help with a full range of financial products including alternatives, annuities, permanent life insurance, and institutional money management, as well as the usual compliment of stocks and bonds, is a better starting place. The next step is to determine your personal risk comfort level, and only then does a product become a part of the solution.

Let's review a few of the options outside of the normal offering of most investment professionals. Alternative investments are generally defined as anything other than a stock or bond. I see the distinction a little differently because stocks and bonds are generally the product of Wall Street, and many non-traded alternatives are the products of Main Street. Alternative investments receive a lot of scrutiny from regulators—and for good cause, as many have limited or no liquidity—but in today's market, illiquidity pays a premium. Simply put, if you do not need access to your funds for a period, you may be able to receive returns well beyond the Morningstar safe estimate of 2.8 percent safe withdrawal rate. Further, the risks of many of these investments are not correlated with the stock or bond markets. It is not advisable to be oversaturated with any investment, including alternatives, but as of this writing, the income available can be substantially more than what is offered by your typical 60 percent securities/40 percent bonds portfolio that is pushed by mainstream advisors and their firms.

Scenario Two: Income Later

Annuities are another product with tight scrutiny by regulators, and there is an entire industry of financial advisors and radio pundits who tout them as having large fees and being a poor place to put money.

Before we address these issues, let's first define the various types of annuity products available. The first we need to discuss is the immediate annuity. There are several options with this type of annuity, but basically you exchange a sum of money for a guaranteed payout that could be for a set number or years or for the life of one or more people. This is similar to a pension payout.

The second type we need to discuss is the fixed annuity. A fixed annuity is an account with an initial lump sum deposit, or a stream of deposits over time. The investment crediting is tied to a stated interest rate which could be adjusted from time to time or guaranteed for a set period.

The third type of annuity we need to discuss is the variable annuity. This type of annuity has underlying investment accounts (mutual funds) and the surrender value of the annuity is always determined by the underlying securities in the sub accounts. This is quite different from a fixed annuity where the credits are guaranteed by contract. The value of this type of plan is that the underlying securities could go up in value over time, and thus increase the monthly income received during the payout phase of the annuity.

The final annuity we need to discuss has been called an indexed annuity, but the correct legal term is a fixed indexed annuity, or FIA for short. These annuities are linked to an outside index and interest is credited based upon the performance of that outside index, which uses one of several crediting methods. The key to understand is that the product is a "fixed indexed" annuity. It has the guarantees of a fixed annuity because the principal is guaranteed and any credits (once received) cannot be lost. This allows for upside potential gains with no chance of market loss.[14]

The other consideration when purchasing an annuity, and the greatest concern of suitability by regulators is that, while you do not pay a charge up front, an early surrender could lead to a loss

---

[14] All annuity payments are based on the claim paying ability of the issuing company, and certain riders do have fees involved.

of principal. Suitability in purchasing an annuity varies from carrier to carrier, but the goal is to ascertain the financial condition of the client, and if a particular annuity is an acceptable fit.

So, does this mean that you give up control of your money to an insurance company in exchange for a lifetime check? A few years ago, that was the norm unless you were simply taking a systematic withdrawal such as a fixed amount of a fixed percentage for each payment from the cash value of the contract. This all began to change about ten years ago with the creation of a new benefit called a Guaranteed Lifetime Withdrawal Benefit (GLWB). The GLWB has been made available on fixed, variable, and fixed indexed annuities—usually for a fee—that varies from carrier to carrier and contract to contract. I have jokingly referred to this rider as the "Boomer Benefit." Boomers have often been accused of wanting our cake and eating it too (I can say this because I am a boomer, as well).

Adding a GLWB rider to an annuity contract essentially allows you to take a set percentage from your account based upon your age at activation, and the payment amount is guaranteed for the life of one or more annuitants. This sounds a lot like an immediate annuity, but there is one critical difference. There is usually no going back to your circumstances prior to the election with an immediate annuity, while with a GLWB, your cash value is still available as a partial withdrawal as long as there remains a balance in the cash account. A withdrawal will reduce your monthly payment amount, but having this option is something that was not available in previous products. Further, if there is any cash value left at the death of the annuitant(s), the balance is paid out to the beneficiary! The GLWB is an example of actuarial arbitrage being used in favor of the annuitant, especially for later income. The longer the income account has the ability to grow, the greater the amount of the guaranteed annual payout.

A few years ago, a new prospective client couple came to see me about their retirement income needs and wanted to know when they would be able to retire. They were both still working, and they planned to work another three to five years. After determining a current budget and a retirement budget, we began the process of working backward to find exactly how much money they were going to need per month. We included methods to maximize Social Security, but unfortunately, they did not qualify for a pension and were very concerned about depending on market-based products to fill their minimum required monthly income. By using the benefits of a GLWB, we were able to grow their future income account by a guaranteed 7 percent per year for four years, and then at age sixty-seven turn on an income stream that amounted to 5.5 percent of their income account value and guaranteed the payment for both of their lives. Since we only used a percentage of their total account value to provide this guaranteed account, we were able to allow the rest of their funds to continue to grow until they were ready to retire (more on that later).

This combination of allocating enough funds to an income account to provide for a guaranteed income made my clients more comfortable to let their growth account continue to grow. In fact, between additional payments into their 401(k), employer matches, and a healthy market, their growth account doubled prior to their planned retirement age. While every situation is unique and what works for one person is certainly not a guarantee for another, this particular client seems to have benefited from this approach and a written financial plan.

Scenario Three: Income Much Later

This next idea for retirement income receives even more pushback from the investment world than annuities. I mean, who in their right mind would consider funding their retirement with permanent life insurance?

Please don't close the book and think that I'm trying to sell life insurance. I'm not. But I do want to give a fair shake to a product that has unique benefits, and when used correctly, may be able to greatly exceed the withdrawal percentage that Morningstar said is a safe percentage and, in some cases, may even beat what can be provided by an annuity with the GLWB rider. What's more, when properly structured, these amounts can be used without taxation.

Let me tell you a story about a client of mine who read a book called *SMART*, which is an acronym for the "Strategic Movement Around Retirement Taxation." The book presented a very convincing case to my client about using permanent life insurance to fund retirement income with payouts that exceeded many of the products he was currently invested in.

Now let me be clear, this client had already maxed out his qualified retirement savings, as well as his Roth IRA, but as a businessman with considerable cash flow, he had additional funds that he wanted to put away for retirement and then ultimately leave to his family.

He approached me after reading the aforementioned book and said, "How can I participate in this?" I had known the client for some time and knew he had experienced some health issues that would not make him a good prospect for life insurance, and I told him that was the case. However, he had children who were in excellent health and ultimately, he wanted his estate to go to them.

After speaking with his family, they agreed to allow him to purchase a very specific type of life insurance on their lives called a Ten-Pay Whole Life policy. The client agreed to put $50,000 per year into the policies on his daughter's life between age forty-seven through fifty-seven, with the intention of letting the funds set for an additional ten years. Assuming current dividends, she would be able to pull over $40,000 per year, tax-free, for her life expectancy. Further, as the owner of the policy, the funds are still available to him, should he need them. The most amazing part of all of this is, if my client does not need the funds and his daughter begins a lifetime income at age sixty-seven through life expectancy, there will still be over one million dollars in death benefits for his grandchildren!

Please understand that his scenario is unusual. However, without proper planning and a professional who understands all your options, you could miss out on ways (like this one) to improve your lifestyle.

S = Safety

I began this chapter with the mantra of many financial advisors: "Don't worry, you're in it for the long haul." I don't disagree with that mantra if retirement is ten-plus years away, but I take issue if I am still being told this and I plan to retire in the next one to ten years. You probably remember a country musician named Kenny Rogers who wrote a song called "The Gambler," famous in the 1970s. The one line that I am always reminded of is, "You gotta know when to hold them, know when to fold them, know when to walk away, and know when to run." If you are going to invest in the market, running is not where you want to be. You want to be in a position to "hold them" when required, and that is not always an option when you are needing retirement income. For this reason, I have found it brings a lot of peace to my clients, and, more importantly gives them the confidence to move forward with a portion of their money in a growth position, if we first create a plan that includes a comfortable amount of money safely tucked away after income needs are met.

A few years ago, I was approached by a client who was insistent that she wanted to pull out 401(k) funds and pay off her mortgage.

After reviewing her current mortgage, we found she had a 2.75 percent, fifteen-year mortgage, and her portfolio was currently averaging over 5 percent with half of her funds in a safe account averaging over 3 percent. To pay off the mortgage would have required her to pull the 3 percent account (as the growth fund was currently experiencing a small correction). I asked why would she even consider cashing in a 3 percent account to pay off a 2.75 percent mortgage and pay taxes at a level much higher than if she did not pay the mortgage off?

I explained she was about to make an emotional decision rather than a mathematical decision and asked for some time to run the numbers and show what I meant. We agreed to meet a few days later. After I had completed a cash flow analysis, I was able to show her that paying off the mortgage all at once would increase her taxes this year, cause her to lose her mortgage deduction in all future years, and give up a quarter percent of earnings on her funds immediately, not to mention the future value of those funds. After our discussion, she agreed that perhaps paying off her home right now was not the best idea.

I make this point not to say you should or should not pay off your home. I make this point to say that it's always better to make a mathematical decision rather than an emotional decision.

So how do we find principal protected "safe" growth accounts? The answer to this question is market innovation.

I am a firm believer in the American free enterprise system. I believe when people are allowed to pursue what is in their own best interests and have the freedom to "vote with their feet" by moving their assets from one investment to another, those companies losing the game will either go out of business or find attractive ways to get those clients and their dollars back.

This is what happened about twenty years ago. Insurance companies could no longer compete with investment firms for client dollars, as their interest rates had been steadily going down for over a decade while the market was setting new records seemingly every week. The old version of their solution was the variable annuity, but as the radio pundits are always pointing out, why would you wrap a mutual fund (with fees) into an insurance product with *more* fees in the hope of increasing your wealth? To get an idea of the cost of fees look at the following chart:

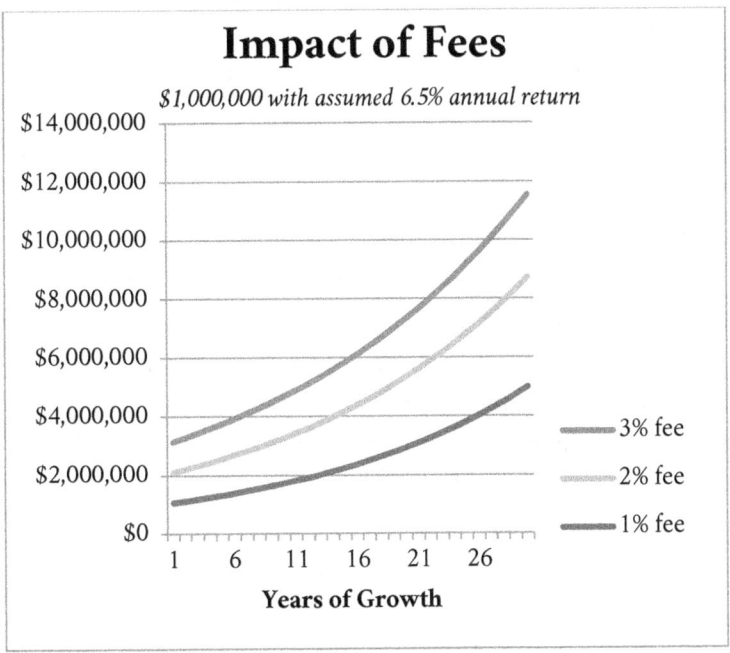

A typical variable annuity includes fees (in addition to the underlying fees of the sub accounts) that could range from 0.5 percent to as much as 4 percent! As you can see from the chart, even a 1 percent fee over a twenty-five-plus-year timeline can cost you an exponential amount of money. So why do people put funds in annuities in the first place and what qualifies them as a safe investment? To understand my thoughts on what is safe, we must look back at history, specifically the Great Depression era.

In 1929, the stock market crashed and set off a crushing series of events for our country. But the market crash was only part of the problem. It was the failure of the banks as a "safe haven" that exacerbated the problem even further. It was the nation's life insurance companies that continued to protect and grow the wealth of those who were invested with them.

Have you ever heard of a baseball player named George Herman Ruth? He is more commonly known as "Babe" Ruth. The Babe had a financial advisor throughout his career who insisted he move much of his earnings into safe products, including life insurance and annuities. When the Babe retired, it is reported that his "safe" investments yielded enough income to maintain a Manhattan apartment and keep up with his notorious spending habits.

His advisor's name was Christy Walsh, and recent articles suggest he not only kept the Babe safe through the Great Depression but is also credited with creating the modern day "agent" to sports celebrities. So why would Christy Walsh move much of the Babe's assets into life insurance and annuities? Perhaps because he understood the underlying business models of banks and insurance companies. The modern-day bank makes its income from loaning money for just about anything you can imagine. Banks depend on an algorithm that is supposed to estimate the likelihood of the repayment of the money they loan out. We know this algorithm as our credit score and the higher the score, the lower the supposed risk to the bank. However, banks make long-term decisions based on short-term information. How can your credit score predict if you will have an income and be able to repay your thirty-year mortgage loan in five years? It simply can't do that.

So, why do we put our safe money in such a risky business? The answer is FDIC guarantees. FDIC stands for Federal Deposit Insurance Corporation, and this institution stands behind your deposits. Why do we have the FDIC? Because banking is a risky business and, in order to feel safe, we want to know that if the bank makes bad loans with our funds, that they have a back-up plan for returning our money. For the past eighty years, this system has served us well, and to date, no one has lost any funds in an FDIC-insured account in spite of 3491 failures and 586 assists between 1934 and 2017. [15]

Let's compare the banking business model to that of a life insurance company offering an annuity product. Insurance companies use a similar algorithm to determine longevity. They are accurate to less than a 1 percent discrepancy. In fact, there is a 100 percent chance that if you are reading this book, you will not get out of this life alive. Not to sound morbid, but the simple truth is that the payout from an annuity is based upon the assured fact that we are all going to eventually die, versus the payout from a bank deposit account's dependence on the repayment of a loan. Don't get me wrong, insurance companies have gone out of business, as well, and you should dig deep into the ratings and financial situation of any product before you spend your money, including annuities, as the return of your money is totally dependent on the claims-paying ability of the company.

My point is simply that making blanket statements that annuities are "bad" is unfair and suspect when many of the people making these statements receive endorsement money from other financial institutions who have a vested interest in demeaning the annuity business. I am a firm believer that just about all financial products are beneficial if they are used correctly. My problem with the approach of many advisory firms is that they have a vested interest in using products that are not necessarily meant for what they are sold to do.

So, what is the final verdict? Where do you put the safe portion of your money? That is not a question that this book can answer, but it is a question you can answer for yourself in conjunction with

---

[15] www.fdic.gov

your financial advisor. Keep your mind open to something more than the noise that is so rampant in our industry.

To find out where to put your safe dollars, you will need to go through a detailed analysis of whatever product you choose. However, to determine how much of your money should be in your Safety bucket, following the Rule of 100 could be a good starting place. We will discuss this further in the next section.

G = Growth

Having your income bucket fully funded to meet your ongoing retirement income needs, plus a comfortable percentage of your assets in the safety bucket, allows you to make mathematical decisions rather than emotional decisions about your growth bucket. Many of my clients over the years have insisted on accepting low returns on all their funds because of previous bad experiences with their growth bucket. This is not uncommon, as many advisors keep *all* a client's assets in the growth bucket, and "hold on, you're in it for the long haul" is their only explanation for doing so!

This is unfortunate, because most of us have a point where we will cry "uncle" and want out of the pain being caused by persistent losses. So, we bail at the wrong time and miss the next bull market, which historically puts us at a new high that was higher than our previous high. You see, markets go up and down based on many factors and not all of them are good indicators of when to decide to bail.

Conversely, certain trends are clear indicators that it's time to take your winnings off the table, especially in retirement. When you are thirty years old and have thirty years of time on your side, using a buy-and-hold strategy may make perfect sense as time is on your side. On the other hand, being age sixty and expecting to live off an account that was designed for a long-term buy-and-hold strategy may not make sense. The possibility of using an annuity for safety or bank deposits with all your money at age sixty may not make sense, either.

While there is no definitive percentage for every person of what should be in the safe bucket or the growth bucket, I have found that an old industry maxim referred to as the "Rule of 100" makes a lot of sense. This rule simply states that if you take the number 100 and subtract your current age, the difference is how much you should have as a percentage of the whole in your safe bucket. For example: Tom is sixty years old. After meeting his income needs, he has $500,000 left to allocate. Based on the Rule of 100, Tom should put $300,000 in his safe bucket and $200,000 in his growth bucket. It really is as simple as that.

Once we know what dollar amount, we need to fund our income and we have tucked away sufficient dollars in our safety bucket to feel comfortable, then (and in my opinion, only then) we should begin to find suitable investments and strategies to fund our growth bucket. So, with the myriad of possibilities available, including: mutual funds, exchange-traded funds (ETFs), managed accounts, index funds, individual stocks, and many others, how do we decide where to put these assets? The first key is to be comfortable with whatever amount of money you place in your growth bucket and realize that this portion can actually be "for the long haul" because your other dollars are properly allocated to investments designed to cover your income needs and give you the security to sleep at night.

With so many options, as an advisor, I must take a position. For my clients, this usually means institutional money managers versus index funds. Long-term dollars in a group of index funds, and properly reallocated at least annually is, without a doubt, one of the lowest-cost ways to grow your wealth and, if you plan to manage your own money, this is the path I would recommend. But if you are going to pay a fee to someone to manage your accounts, I believe you should be getting your money's worth.[16]

In a nutshell, the funds that we allocate to our growth bucket are our hedge against future inflation and for this reason we need to expect and get outsized returns over time with as little correlation to the overall market as possible. This is difficult for the average investor to accomplish when managing his own funds. Frankly, it would be difficult for most advisors to accomplish as well, with all the other duties and responsibilities required to manage and grow a financial firm. Many of my clients have benefited from institutional money management. To be completely transparent, institutional money management comes with minimum account sizes and will not be available to every investor. If that is the case, an indexed approach or a family of mutual funds may be the best idea. But for those who can maintain a sufficient balance to qualify for ongoing institutional management, the upside and long-term potential for growth is exceptional.

If you used the analogy of a football team to describe this approach, it would look like this: You (the investor) are the owner of the team. You provide the facility to hold the games, pay the referees, and the coach. The coach in this analogy is your advisor. His job is to find the right players (money managers) to achieve the winning game plan that meets the owner's expectations. It is the coach's responsibility to find, retain, and if necessary, fire the players who do not meet the standards of the team owner. There are several additional reasons to hire outside talent to work with your growth bucket. Let's look at a few:

---

[16] Information provided in this book is intended for educational purposes only and should not mistake as an offer to render personalized investment advice or financial planning advice.

- First, planning this way involves less emotion and more strategy (assuming your two other buckets have been properly funded).
- Second, it involves professional oversight on a daily basis with each piece of your growth bucket being managed according to the specifics you and your manager have agreed on.
- You'll have no ongoing sales commissions or trading costs (assuming you have negotiated a true wrap-fee account).
- You'll have full liquidity on this portion of your plan. No long-term commitments. You can fire the manager at any time if they are not meeting your needs and if you don't have a commission that must be recouped.
- Finally, individual needs can be custom-tailored by allocating differing percentages to multiple managers, thus giving you a chance to benefit from more than one strategy.

This list could be much longer, but I hope you see why I believe institutional money management or indexed investing as being the best choice for your growth bucket. It may seem strange to an investor who has spent the last forty years trying to grow wealth to focus on the growth bucket last. After all, we have been schooled for years that inflation will eat up our future if we don't focus on growth. While it's true that inflation is a silent thief and continues into retirement, there is a fundamental shift that occurs when we begin to live off the investments that we have spent a lifetime building. The shift that I am referencing has to do with focusing on a danger much worse than inflation, and that danger is taxation.

As a retiree, managing our taxes becomes paramount to our success. Let's face it, 3 percent inflation is almost nothing compared to 20 percent taxation. So, let's continue with our process understanding that growth is indeed our future inflation bucket, but part three of our process, tax planning, is where returns much greater than growth may likely be found.

Part Two: Action Items

1. Determine how much of your funds should be allocated to each of the three buckets: I = Income, S = Safety, G = Growth.
2. Consider income-generating assets for your income bucket such as alternative investments. You can request our free report on alternative investments at www.sokyadvisors.com.
3. Consider principal-protected assets for the safety bucket that also have the potential to exceed inflation rates. Market-linked assets may be a possibility.
4. Consider the costs of institutional money management versus indexed investing. Using a team approach may produce the most efficient returns, and if your current team is not making money for you, find a new team.
5. Interview multiple advisors until you find one who offers more than the standard "you're in it for the long haul" or "the market's down, you should buy more" mantras touted by most of the investment community.

PART THREE

Tax Planning

"Government's view of the economy could be summed up in a few short phrases: If it moves, tax it. If it keeps moving, regulate it. And if it stops moving, subsidize it."

-Ronald Reagan

In his book *The Creature from Jekyll Island*, author G. Edward Griffin tells a story of how an elite group of bankers and industrialists met to craft what would become the 16th Amendment to the United States Constitution. This amendment was ratified on December 23, 1913, by the United States Senate and signed into by law by then-president Woodrow Wilson. The ratification of the 16th Amendment made it possible for Congress to create what would become the Internal Revenue Service and the Federal Reserve Bank. The Internal Revenue Service was established as the tax-collections arm of the government and the Federal Reserve Bank as a quasi-government branch charged with the monetary policy of our country. I use the term quasi-government, but the Federal Reserve Bank of Saint Louis defines the institution as follows:

"The Federal Reserve Banks are *not* a part of the federal government, but they exist because of an *act of Congress*. Their purpose is to serve the public."

So, is the Fed private or public?

The answer is both. While the Board of Governors is an independent government agency, the Federal Reserve Banks are set up like private corporations. Member banks hold stock in the Federal Reserve Banks and earn dividends. Holding this stock does not carry with it the control and financial interest given to holders of common stock in for-profit organizations. The stock may not be sold or pledged as collateral for loans. Member banks also appoint six of the nine members of each Bank's board of directors." [17]

Prior to the ratification of the 16th Amendment, our Constitution did not allow for a permanent taxation of income, but this amendment paved the way for our modern-day tax system. Whether you believe the account told by G. Edward Griffin in his book mentioned above or not, the fact remains that for the past hundred-plus years, taxes and how to deal with them most efficiently have become critical issues in the making of financial decisions and is especially critical to those entering retirement. The simple truth is that tax preparation and tax planning are two separate and distinct disciplines. And while both are necessary, tax planning will determine what is left for the tax preparer to report. I personally agree with the statement by Judge Learned Hand, the most often-quoted lower court judge in history. Judge Hand was a profound legal scholar, but my favorite quote is as follows:

> "Anyone may arrange his affairs so that his taxes shall be as low as possible; he is not bound to choose that pattern which best pays the treasury. There is not even a patriotic duty to increase one's taxes. Over and over again the Courts have said that there is nothing sinister in so arranging affairs as to keep taxes as low as possible. Everyone does it, rich and poor alike and all do right, for nobody owes any public duty to pay more than the law demands."

---

[17] Federal Reserve Bank of St. Louis. "Who Owns Reserve Banks?" https://www.stlouisfed.org/in-plain-english/who-owns-the-federal-reserve-banks

In Part Three of this book, our focus will be on "the arranging of our affairs" in retirement to pay as little tax as is required by law. For many retirees, the biggest tax exposure comes when they have a partner who owns a good chunk of the retirement savings, they think is theirs. The truth is, they only own a portion of the qualified funds, such as 401(k), 403(b), and IRA accounts they are depending on to supplement their income in retirement. Legal tax avoidance is a critical part in structuring your own New Retirement Blueprint as there are few things you can do that provide greater returns than managing your tax burden as efficiently as possible. Below I'd like to share a short story that succinctly outlines the issue.

> *Once upon a time in a small rural town, the local magistrate was given authority by the king to offer his subjects who worked in agriculture a choice on how to pay their taxes. The magistrate called a town meeting of all the farmers and explained the two options that the king was offering. Option One was a tax established today that would require 20 percent of each farmer's seed prior to planting their crop. Option Two was presented as a deferral of taxes until after the harvest at which time the king would determine what percentage of the harvest he would require. The magistrate advised the farmers that the king would allow them one week to discuss among themselves and their families and he would return to the meeting hall to receive each farmer's decision. He elaborated that each farmer could choose which method of taxation was best for them, but once their decision was made, the king would not allow them to make a change without severe penalties. He also advised that if you decided to pay the tax from the seed, it would be taken at the next meeting and to be prepared that day to pay the tax. The meeting was adjourned, but two of the farmers, Haman and Mordecai, decided to continue the conversation at the local pub.*
>
> *Haman began the conversation. "Mordecai, what do you think is the right decision concerning the king's two options?"*
>
> *Mordecai thought for a moment and answered, "Haman, I believe the king's intent is good, but since I do not possess a crystal ball and can't see*

the future, I am going to pay my tax at the next meeting." Haman protested, "But what if the harvest were to fail? Then you would have paid in vain. Besides, you know the king is gracious and only taxes what he needs. I believe I will wait and pay my tax at the harvest when taxes will most likely be less than today." Mordecai lifted his pint and said, "Good luck to you my friend. I guess we will have to wait and see which decision works out best."

So, the farmers went their separate ways and the following week each man acted in accordance with the decision they had made in the pub. Mordecai paid the king 20 percent of his seed, and Haman deferred his payment until the harvest. Time passed, and life continued for both farmers. One day a messenger from the king came to the town and announced that the king had decided to start a war with a neighboring country, but not to worry, the king had decided to borrow the funds and no taxes would be required. Sometime later another messenger arrived and gave the town great news, that the king had been persuaded to provide free health care for all the citizens, but not to worry, the king had found a way to fund his idea by reducing payments to the physicians and had found a new creditor from the far east who was willing to loan the king the difference required to provide this benefit to the people. So, the people enjoyed the free health care and other benefits the king had bestowed upon them in his graciousness.

Time passed and the harvest came. It was abundant, and the people were amazed at their returns. In fact, most of the farmers were now millionaires and they were overjoyed with their good fortune and looked forward to what they would do with their extra money. They planned on traveling and providing gifts for their grandchildren, and possibly buying a second home in the mountainous regions to the east, or a beach home in the southern region of the country.

The month after the harvest, the magistrate arrived in the town with hundreds of wagons and horses and soldiers. He called a town meeting and requested all to attend. Once the people were all assembled, he read a list of people and ask them to stand up. He advised the people from the first list, that the king in his graciousness wanted to thank them for the seed they provided some time ago and told them they were free to leave and enjoy the *fruit of their labor. Mordecai and the others who had paid their tax beforehand thanked the magistrate and left the meeting.*

The magistrate then turned to the crowd and congratulated them on their record-setting harvest. He then passed out an edict from the king, which showed the total debt the king had incurred over the past months and the accumulated interest from the loans he had secured to fight his wars and provide for the people. Haman raised his hand and asked the magistrate why he had brought all the wagons, horses and soldiers. The magistrate assured Haman and the rest of the crowd that there was nothing to be concerned about. He was simply there to collect the king's tax on the harvest. Haman asked the magistrate what percentage the king would expect at this time, and the magistrate replied only a fair amount. The people were quite alarmed and pushed the magistrate for an answer. The magistrate pointed to the edict and explained that the king had borrowed heavily and would need to repay the debt as well as the interest and would need 40 percent of the harvest in order to continue his government.

The people were shocked and angry, as they had assumed their taxes would be less at this time, when in fact the taxes were double what they had been before the king's spending on wars and benefits for the people. As the crowd continued to become more agitated, the people realized they were no match for the king and his tax collectors. The crowd disbanded each person to his own farm to gather the king's share and load the king's wagons with their hard-earned crops.

If you are like many Americans, you have a partnership with the king. The partnership is represented by your qualified retirement accounts such as 401(k), 403(b), and IRA. You probably believed, as I did, that surely taxes would be lower in retirement and thus deferring tax until "after the harvest" made a lot of sense. The problem is that most of us did not take the time to study the history of taxation in the United States. Look at the following chart.

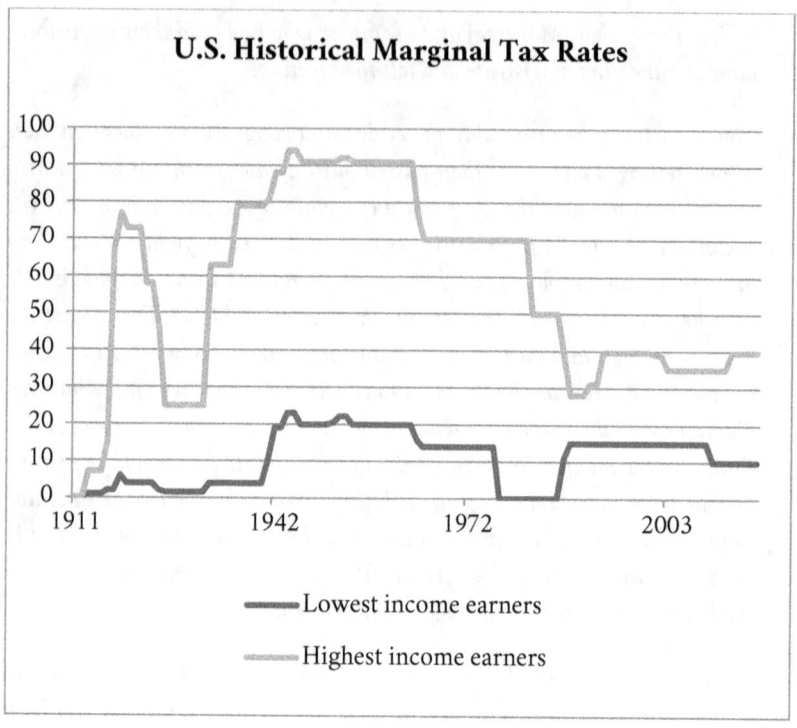

As you can see, at the starting point back in 1913, the income tax rate was extremely low as the promoters had promised it would be and it primarily affected the "rich" which was the way the amendment was sold to the public in the first place. For those who think the idea of "soaking the rich" is a new one, let me assure you it is at least as old as the tax system itself. The problem in "soaking the rich" is in who decides who the "rich" are. By 1945, the "rich" was anyone who earned more than $200,000, and our government wanted over 90 percent of any amount over that![18]

The history of American income taxation shows broad increases following the various wars that were fought all the way through the Vietnam war. However, the tax rates following the

---

[18] Tax Policy Center. https://www.taxpolicycenter.org/statistics/historical-highest-marginal-income-tax-rates.

Gulf War and the invasion of Iraq are some of the lowest seen in in the hundred-year time span. If you compare this timeline with the accumulation of debt in our country, you will see that the last two conflicts were fought with debt rather than taxes.[19]

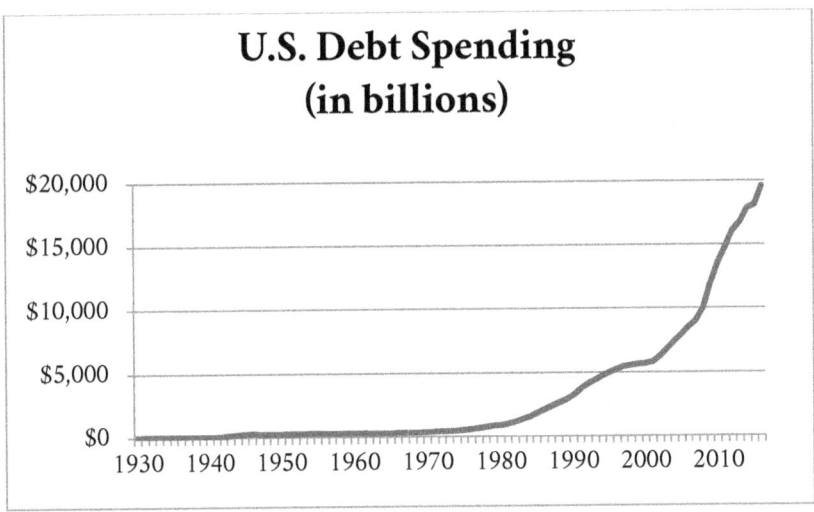

I wish I could say that the debt shown in the previous chart was all we had to worry about. However, the next chart shows the increase in debt to GDP (GDP stands for the gross domestic product of a nation. It is the sum of all goods and services produced) from 2006 to 2014. On January 1st, 2008, a monumental event happened in America, and it's continued since then at a rapid pace and will continue for about another ten years. What happened on that date? The very first "baby boomer" turned sixty-two and qualified for Social Security benefits. Three years later, the first boomer qualified for Medicare and full Social Security benefits. As you can see from the following chart, the percentage of debt to GDP grew

---

[19] U.S. Government Spending. https://www.usgovernmentspending.com/debt_deficit_history

precipitously for the years following this event and continues to this day. [20]

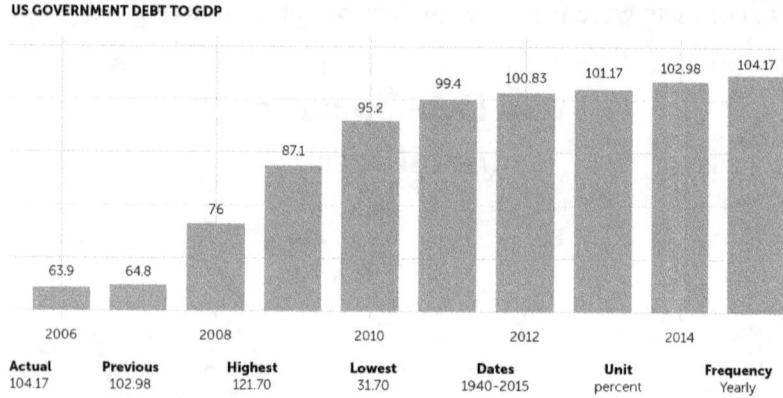

Generally, Government debt as a percent of GDP is used by investors to measure a country ability to make future payments on its debt, thus affecting the country borrowing costs and government bond yields. This page provides - United States Government Debt to GDP - actual values, historical data, forecast, chart, statistics, economic calendar and news. United States Government Debt to GDP - actual data, historical chart and calendar of releases - was last updated on August of 2016.

Many will lament this problem by stating the obvious: that Social Security was robbed by the politicians, and while it is true the funds were borrowed and became a part of the national debt, the real issue is not the amount already borrowed, but rather the amount that must continue to be borrowed or taxed to give the benefits already promised.

There is a point where taxation hinders a person's will to work, and with an estimate of only three people paying for every one person drawing within the next decade, we certainly can't afford to discourage the current population by taxing them to the point of losing their incentive to work.

So, where do these funds come from? I believe you know the answer just as the farmers in the story knew the answer to their

---

[20] Trading Economics. U.S. Bureau of Public Debt. https://tradingeconomics.com/united-states/government-debt-to-gdp

tax issue. It's coming from your harvest. It's coming from the taxation of your Social Security benefits, reduced payments to Medicare, and your qualified plan distributions. There is no doubt the Gen-Xers and millennials will be taxed more, and their eventual benefits will be further down the road than what was originally promised through pushing back eligibility ages. I wish that would be enough, but it will not be. According to the Investment Company Institute, there is as of this writing $29.2 trillion dollars in qualified accounts.[21] If we assume the Treasury eventually winds up with 20 percent of this amount, that is almost $6 trillion in taxes that will be paid by retirees.

There is a large ray of sunshine amongst some of this negativity. As of this writing, we are entering a period of the lowest taxes in most baby boomers' adult lives. With the passing of the Tax Cuts and Job Acts of 2017, there's a good chance there will be a continual lower tax rate for the next six years. In other words, now may be the time to take whatever action that is best for your situation. It is unlikely that we will see taxes this low again in our lifetimes.

How will retirees be taxed on these funds? For those who don't act, the first way is the most obvious: an eventual higher tax rate. The other ways are not as obvious. Higher medical payments on Medicare (for example, since 1965, the initial hospital deductible has risen from $40 to $1,484 in 2021),[22] lower Social Security annual increases, higher Part B and D premiums, means testing to receive benefits, and the taxation of Social Security through the provisional income test.

---

[21] Investment Company Institute. December 20, 2018. "Retirement Assets Total $29.2 Trillion in Third Quarter."
https://www.ici.org/research/stats/retirement/ret_18_q3
[22] Ibid.

One of the biggest surprises for many retirees is that upon reaching retirement they no longer have any itemized deductions. Consider these examples:

- No more dependents, as children are usually grown
- No more mortgage interest (unless you still owe for your home)
- No more qualified plan contributions (only earned income can be put into qualified plans)
- No more flex accounts or health savings accounts (HAS) contributions
- No more student loan interest

The loss of these deductions means it is essential to plan to maximize what benefits are still available.

Since the scope of this book is focused on taxes in retirement, the balance of Part Three will discuss the taxation of Social Security through the provisional income test and how to reduce the amount of income that one must report as provisional income. Please be advised that I am in no way providing tax advice for the reader. Every situation is different and should be discussed with your tax professional. The ideas presented may not be for every taxpayer. Yet, this is general information that could be beneficial to discuss with your tax planner and financial advisor when you are making decisions that might affect your future taxability.

As explained in Part One, the taxation of Social Security was originally promised to never happen. And for decades it was not taxed, until 1984. If there is anything that our government seems to be truly bipartisan about, it must be the passage of new taxes. I don't think either political party has ever met a tax they didn't like! But one must remember that those who pass the tax laws must live with them as well. If you oversaw setting the tax laws, and they were going to affect you as well, wouldn't you leave yourself a back door?

I have always believed that taxes are a necessary and important part of a civilized society and I do not condone anyone violating the law as it is written and enforced. I do, however, believe the code was written with the idea that most people would not take the time to understand the code or do the math to make the best decisions. I said earlier that making a mathematical decision and not an emotional decision was a key to success, and when it comes to taxes nothing could be truer. Let's dig in and see where we can reap some rewards for our time spent together by laying out some strategies for successful tax planning.

All personal taxes are filed on some version of form 1040 (see the preceding sample). The line of most concern on IRS form 1040 for most taxpayers is line 22, the amount you owe. However, it is line 7 that should be of greatest concern, because by the time you get to line 22 there is nothing more to do except write the check!

Line 7 is your *adjusted gross income* amount, and it is from this number that all calculations of phase out amounts are made. More importantly, this is the number used by the government to determine any amounts that may be eligible for standard or itemized deductions or phase out of said deductions. The problem with depending on the deductions to reduce your taxable income is that this is where Congress has historically done the most tinkering and changes. The Tax Cuts and Jobs Act of 2017 made changes in this area which were beneficial for most retirees. A couple over the age of sixty-five can now deduct $26,600 from their adjusted gross income. For many retirees who have lost the ability to deduct many of the itemized deductions previously available, this new standard deduction may be of tremendous value to use as an offset against potential Roth conversions (more on this later).

For most retirees who have no W2 income, do not immediately own a business or farm, or have rental property, it is lines 2 through 4 and schedules B and D that will primarily affect your taxation. Line 5a is where you include your Social Security income. Line 5b is where you include the *taxable* portion of your Social Security income. The key to lines 2 through 4 and schedules B and D is to *not* have anything to report.

It is possible to arrange your affairs in such a way as to have nothing to report. For example, if you are receiving 1099 interest on a bank deposit, you will receive a 1099 regardless of what you did with the interest. However, if you chose to put those funds in a tax-deferred account and in other various insurance products that receive no 1099, then your earnings could be deferred indefinitely during your lifetime and possibly pass tax-free to your children. Another way to not have anything to eventually report is to convert qualified accounts to a Roth. In doing so, you will have taxes in the year of conversion, but all earnings and future distributions thereafter will be tax-free. One way to maximize the current standard deduction mentioned before would be to do sufficient Roth conversions each year to maximize the standard deduction. To not do so is wasting the legal benefits provided by the tax code. Please note Roth conversions are a complicated matter and should not be done without consultation with a tax professional, but please consult with your tax professional about ways to maximize this opportunity during the current low tax environment that we currently have. The federal tax rates after the Tax Cuts and Job Act of 2017 are listed in the following chart. As you can see, for a married couple, up to $77,400 of taxable income only requires a maximum of 12 percent federal taxation at this time. One might say that taxes are on sale as of this writing! This example is based on married filing jointly status. Other filers may have different brackets.

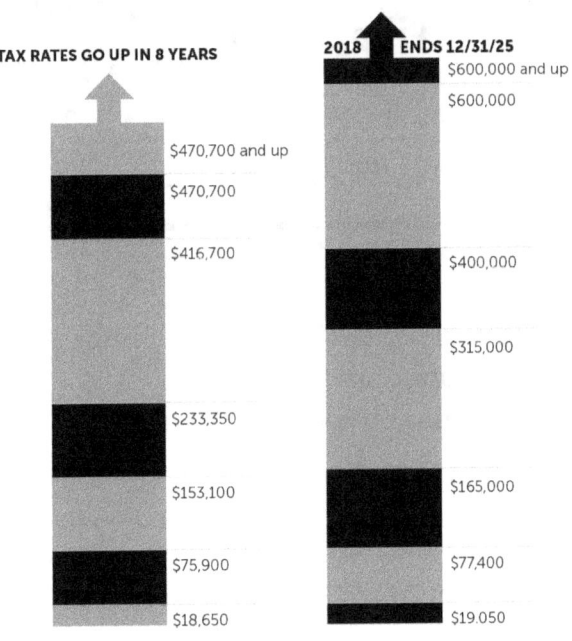

The provisional income tax is calculated by taking all items in lines 1 through 4 of your form 1040, plus any income on additional schedules (generally A through F) and adding in 50 percent of your total Social Security benefit. If this number exceeds the limits shown in the provisional tax graph below, then either 50 percent or 85 percent of your Social Security benefit amount goes on line 5b of the return. Please don't try to make this assumption by yourself. A qualified tax professional should be consulted. However, don't make the mistake of assuming you have no choices and do nothing. Take action today and see what your options are. If taxes are raised in the future, you may look back at this time period and wish you had taken advantage of the historically low rates we are currently experiencing.[23]

Social Security Provisional Tax Chart[24]

Single	Married, Filing Jointly	% of Benefits are Taxable
$0 - $25K	$0 - $32K	0%
Above $25K	Above $32K	50%
Above $34K	Above $44K	85%

In the words of Forrest Gump, I guess that's about all I've got to say about that. Please don't put off exploring your options regarding reducing future taxation.

The IRS is counting on your procrastination!

---

[23] Tax Policy Center. https://www.taxpolicycenter.org/statistics/historical-highest-marginal-income-tax-rates.
[24] https://socialsecurityintelligence.com/taxes-on-social-security/

Part Three: Action Items

1. Taxes are on sale right now. It's time to make decisions.
2. Provisional income taxes may be reduced. Find out how.
3. Set an appointment with your tax advisor and get his opinion.
4. Taxes are good and necessary, but you have no obligation to pay more than the law requires.

PART FOUR

Health Care Planning

"No longer will older Americans be denied the healing miracle of modern medicine..."

-Lyndon B. Johnson

In an earlier section I referenced a conversation I had with my grandfather regarding the three-legged stool. I spent much of my childhood with my grandparents. They lived at the end of a dirt road that was unpassable in the winter or after a heavy rain without a tractor. I spent many nights during the school year staying with my grandparents, and most of my summer vacation. When I stayed for the summer, we only went to town once per week and spent most days working in the tobacco patch, hauling hay and milking the cows. It was a blissful time in my life, and I am very thankful for having had the opportunity to learn from my family's decades of wisdom.

One summer night as we sat on the front porch and listened to the coyote's howl in the field just in front of the old house, my grandfather started a conversation about the passage of a law that he referred to as "insurance for old people." He was a devout conservative and even though he benefited greatly from the care provided to him by Medicare, he had been opposed to the passage of the law. As a child, I had no idea at the time about the politics behind the passing of the law, but our conversation that night was one I never forgot. Granddad told me that providing health care for the elderly would eventually get too expensive to maintain. His reasoning was that people would abuse the program through overusing the benefits, and doctors would get rich from it. Therefore, it would eventually get too expensive to continue. For a man without a lot of formal education, he had plenty of what the country folks called "horse sense," or what we would probably call "common sense" today. His thoughts have played out in their entirety over the past fifty years. Utilization has increased exponentially, medical inflation has been higher than any other industry, and today the health care industry accounts for almost 20 percent of our gross domestic product. So, what was the history behind the creation of this program, and what did its founders hope to accomplish?

It was President Lyndon B. Johnson who implemented the first rendition of what we know as the Medicare and Social Security Amendments of 1965. This also brought Medicare and Medicaid into the mix, which was our country's first taste of socialized medicine. With this implementation came backlash, and eventually the expense of maintaining these programs cost much more than what many hoped.

Most of the backlash of this program came from medical professionals. Their opposition resulted in a lot of public protest. Previously, Harry Truman tried to propose a similar deal that would further send the United States into a more socialized medical system, but after World War Two there was little, he could do because of the public's resistance to the idea.

The idea for a bill that would revamp the health care system was seriously considered near the end of World War Two. Three politicians, Senator Robert Wagner, Senator James Murray, and Representative John Dingell fought to bring this bill—called the

Wagner, Murray, Dingell Bill—into fruition in 1943. This bill would have completely revamped the Social Security Act, which would allow for a brand-new health insurance system for the whole country. Despite Wagner, Murray, and Dingell's efforts, however, the bill was never highly considered in Washington.

Although the bill was not considered at the time, President Roosevelt did his best to bring the bill back into the public eye. He died before action was taken, and the new President Truman picked up the momentum, advocating for the WMD Bill. He fought for the bill in spite of the disapproval of politicians and citizens, particularly the majority of medical professionals at the time.

In the end, however, Truman was unable to make the bill a reality. He couldn't simply ignore the blatant disapproval from the rest of the United States, especially after the American Medical Association launched a $1.5 million campaign advocating the eradication of a system of socialized medicine. This campaign included massive spending on advertisements stating, "guard your health, guard your pocketbook; socialized medicine would rob both."

At this point, there wasn't much Truman could do.

After that fiasco, the government's focus shifted to rebuilding the economy. As efforts were made to continue life as it was, the Cold War began. Many might assume that the idea of a socialized health care system was placed on the backburner during this time, but it actually stayed in the public eye throughout this time. Why? Because more elderly citizens were worried about how health care would impact their finances.

President Johnson decided to refocus the country's priorities in 1965 through a speech delivered to Congress called "Advancing the Nation's Health." This speech asked that the United States develop a new insurance program for the elderly, as well as impoverished children. This speech was considered by Congress and eventually they implemented the Social Security Amendments of 1965.

Congress explained in the bill that its purpose was "to provide a hospital insurance program for the aged under the Social Security Act, with a supplementary health benefits program and an expanded program of medical assistance, to increase benefits under the old-age, survivors, and disability insurance system, to improve the federal-state public assistance program, and for other purposes."[25]

This time, despite the consistent disapproval of the American Medical Association and other United States citizens, this legislation was still approved and signed by President Johnson, with Truman watching. After years of work to implement a new national health insurance system to benefit older Americans, Truman finally saw his wish granted.

In August 1965, right after the legislation was signed, 18 million people were eligible for Medicare. A few months later in March 1966, 17 million of those people were enrolled. In May of that same year, the remaining million were enrolled. July 1, 1966 was the day this new medical service was available to everyone enrolled.

At this point, Medicare was still very young, and it wasn't exactly what we know it to be today. When it was first born, Medicare provided only hospital insurance and medical insurance, which is about equivalent to the modern Part A and Part B. Now, more than fifty years later, several amendments have been applied to Medicare, ironing out the wrinkles and introducing Part C and Part D.

It's estimated that total Medicare enrollment will be more than 80 million individuals by the year 2030. Medicaid, too, is seeing

---

[25] United States, Social Security Administration. Archive. "Social Security Amendments of 1965." https://archive.org/details/socialsecurityam00unit_4

an increase in customers because of recent implementations like the Patient Protection and Affordable Care Act. There have been many more changes throughout the years, though. Here are a few:

- President Truman, who supported the Social Security Board's recommendation in 1945 for health insurance for beneficiaries, receives the first Medicare card during the July 30, 1965, signing ceremony by President Johnson.
- More than 19 million Americans are enrolled when Medicare takes effect July 1, 1966.
- Individuals younger than sixty-five with disabilities and those with end-stage renal (kidney) disease become eligible for Medicare in 1972.
- In 1980, home health services coverage is broadened, and Medicare supplemental insurance comes under federal oversight.
- In 1983, Medicare covers patients who opt to receive hospice services at home rather than in an institution.
- Nursing home residents get better protections in 1987.
- Several significant changes happen in 1988, including better hospital and skilled nursing benefits and mammogram coverage. Some changes, such as limited drug benefits and caps on out-of-pocket expenses, are protested by patients and repealed the next year.
- President George H.W. Bush signs legislations for what becomes known as Medicare Part D, which provides prescription drug benefits. About 25 percent of Medicare beneficiaries didn't have drug benefits before Part D.
- The 1990s brought greater enrollments in Medicare and expanded Medicare and Medicaid coverage for low-income individuals, including having Medicaid pay premiums for Medicare beneficiaries with incomes at 100 to 120 percent of the poverty levels. More standards for supplemental insurance are put in place. Private market options

for additional supplemental insurance (Medicare Part C) and prescription drug benefits become available through Medicare Plus choice plans.

- By 1997, more changes happened to Medicare, including providing education and information help for beneficiaries to make informed choices about care.
- In 1998, the website medicare.gov is launched.
- The Patient Protection and Affordable Care Act (ACA) is signed by President Obama in 2010 and brings several reforms, expanded drug and preventative services benefits to Medicare.
- From 2015 to 2018, several changes happened with Medicare, reports the Centers for Medicare & Medicaid Services, of CMS. CMS is focusing more on quality of care by setting payment guidelines that are causing the health care industry to change some delivery models. This ensures that repeat hospitalizations for conditions are reduced. The ACA helped shrink drug costs for beneficiaries who were in the so-called Donut Hole, which will be eliminated by 2020. Premiums for Part B have increased, with the average monthly cost at around $130. CMS also reported that in 2018, 58.5 million people were enrolled in Medicare.

In order to fully understand the subject of health care planning, we must first look at the different components that make up our health care system. In the 1960s with the passage of Medicare, the focus was on inpatient hospital care and physician charges. This was consistent with the health care provided by most commercial carriers at that time. Over time, "health care planning" grew to include coverage for nursing home care, home health care, hospice care, prescription drugs, wellness care, and recovery care. The rise of additional types of care provided by private insurance and

Medicare, plus the impact of increased usage has put in motion a spending frenzy that has pushed the cost of health care in the United States from $146 per person in 1960 to $10,739 per person in 2017. (see the following chart).

Health Care Costs by Year[26,27,28]

Year	National Health Spending (Billions)	Percent Growth	Cost Per Person	Event
1960	$27.2	NA	$146	Recession
1961	$29.1	7.1%	$154	Recession ended
1962	$31.8	9.3%	$166	
1963	$34.6	8.6%	$178	
1964	$38.4	11.0%	$194	LBJ started Medicare and Medicaid
1965	$41.9	9.0%	$209	
1966	$46.1	10.1%	$228	Vietnam War
1967	$51.6	11.9%	$253	
1968	$58.4	13.3%	$284	
1969	$65.9	12.9%	$318	
1970	$74.6	13.1%	$355	Recession
1971	$82.7	11.0%	$389	Wage-price controls
1972	$92.7	12.0%	$431	Stagflation
1973	$102.8	11.0%	$474	Gold standard ended. HMO Act
1974	$116.5	13.4%	$534	ERISA. Wage-price controls ended.
1975	$133.3	14.4%	$605	Inflation at 6.9%
1976	$152.7	14.6%	$688	Inflation at 4.9%
1977	$173.9	13.8%	$777	Inflation at 6.7%

---

[26] Centers for Medicare and Medicaid Services. "Historical." https://www.cms.gov/Research-Statistics-Data-and-Systems/Statistics-Trends-and-Reports/NationalHealthExpendData/NationalHealthAccountsHistorical.html.
[27] The Balance. February 28, 2019. "US Inflation Rate by Year from 1929 to 2020." https://www.thebalance.com/u-s-inflation-rate-history-by-year-and-forecast-3306093
[28] Josh Cothran. California Health Care Foundation. April 6, 2018. "US Health Care Spending: Who Pays? https://www.chcf.org/publication/us-health-care-spending-who-pays/

Year				
1978	$195.3	12.4%	$865	Inflation at 9%
1979	$221.5	13.4%	$971	Inflation at 13.3%
1980	$255.3	15.3%	$1,108	Inflation at 12.5%
1981	$296.2	16.0%	$1,273	Fed raised rates
1982	$334.0	12.8%	$1,422	Recession ended
1983	$367.8	10.1%	$1,550	Tax hike and higher defense spending
1984	$405.0	10.1%	$1,692	
1985	$442.9	9.4%	$1,833	
1986	$474.7	7.2%	$1,947	Tax cut
1987	$516.5	8.8%	$2,099	Black Monday
1988	$579.3	12.2%	$2,332	Fed raised rate
1989	$644.8	11.3%	$2,571	S&L crisis
1990	$721.4	11.9%	$2,843	Recession. Inflation at 6.1%
1991	$788.1	9.2%	$3,070	Recession
1992	$854.1	8.4%	$3,287	
1993	$916.6	7.3%	$3,487	HMOs
1994	$967.2	5.5%	$3,641	
1995	$1,021.6	5.6%	$3,806	Fed raised rate
1996	$1,074.4	5.2%	$3,964	Welfare reform
1997	$1,135.5	5.7%	$4,147	Balanced Budget Act
1998	$1,202.0	5.8%	$4,345	LTCM crisis
1999	$1,278.3	6.4%	$4,576	BBRA
2000	$1,369.7	7.1%	$4,857	BIPA
2001	$1,486.8	8.5%	$5,220	9/11 attacks
2002	$1,629.2	9.6%	$5,668	War on Terror
2003	$1,768.2	8.5%	$6,098	Medicare Modernization Act
2004	$1,896.3	7.2%	$6,481	
2005	$2,024.2	6.7%	$6,855	Bankruptcy Act
2006	$2,156.5	6.5%	$7,233	
2007	$2,295.7	6.5%	$7,628	Inflation at 4.1%
2008	$2,399.1	4.5%	$7,897	Recession slowed spending.
2009	$2,495.4	4.0%	$8,143	
2010	$2,598.8	4.1%	$8,412	ACA signed.
2011	$2,689.3	3.5%	$8,644	Debt crisis
2012	$2,797.3	4.0%	$8,924	Fiscal cliff
2013	$2,879.0	2.9%	$9,121	ACA taxes
2014	$3,026.2	5.1%	$9,515	Exchanges opened.
2015	$3,200.8	5.8%	$9,994	
2016	$3,337.2	4.3%	$10,348	
2017	$3,492.1	3.9%	$10,739	Drug costs rose just 0.4%.

Of the $3.3 trillion spent on health care in 2016, a recent Morningstar report estimates that more than $225 billion was spent on long-term health care in 2015,[29] and The Centers for Medicare and Medicaid Services confirms that Medicare and Medicaid payments exceeded $163 billion on nursing care facilities and continuing care retirement communities in 2016.[30] This would indicate that an excess of $60 billion per year is being spent by private insurance and/or private payments from individuals. To put this in perspective, the national average cost for a year in a nursing home is about $85,000. Look at the following information from www.longtermcare.gov. You can check your state on that site as well.

- $225 a day or $6,844 per month for a semi-private room in a nursing home
- $253 a day or $7,698 per month for a private room in a nursing home
- $119 a day or $3,628 per month for care in an assisted living facility (for a one-bedroom unit)
- $20.50 an hour for a health aide
- $20 an hour for homemaker services
- $68 per day for services in an adult day health care center

The cost of long-term care depends on the type and duration of care you need, the provider you use, and where you live. Costs can be affected by certain factors, such as:

---

[29] Christine Benz. Morningstar. August 31, 2017. "75 Must-Know Statistics about Long-Term Care." https://www.morningstar.com/articles/823957/75-mustknow-statistics-about-longterm-care.html

[30] Emily Mongan. McKnight's Long-Term Care News. December 7, 2017. "National Long-Term Care Spending Hits All-Time High at $163 Billion." https://www.mcknights.com/news/national-long-term-care-spending-hits-all-time-high-at-163-billion/

- Time of day. Home health and home care services, provided in two-to-four-hour blocks of time referred to as "visits," are generally more expensive in the evening, on weekends, and on holidays
- Extra charges for services provided beyond the basic room, food, and housekeeping charges at facilities, although some may have "all inclusive" fees.
- Variable rates in some community programs, such as adult day service, are provided at a per-day rate, but can be more based on extra events and activities."[31]

So where does a retiree start and who do they turn to for help? There are state agencies available for assistance in most states, and there are professionals who are qualified and certified to help with many areas of concern. My first recommendation is that you start planning for health care while you are working on an income plan. Health care is likely to be one of your primary expenses in retirement and paying for it will require sufficient income or assets. A recent report by Vanguard says, "Our model suggests that a medium-risk sixty-five-year-old woman living in a median-cost area, using only traditional Medicare with Part D, could expect to pay between $3,200 and $6,600 for premiums and out-of-pocket medical, dental, and vision costs in 2018 (Figure 1). At the median, she could expect to pay about $3,900."[32] This article is well worth the read and was recently available at the link in the footnote.

Since income planning is the cornerstone of your financial plan, you must be sure that you include estimated annual health care costs in your plan, as well as a plan for potential long-term

---

[31] LongTermCare.Gov. 2016. "Costs of Care." https://longtermcare.acl.gov/costs-how-to-pay/costs-of-care.html

[32] Guyton, et al. Vanguard. June 2018. "Planning for Health Care Costs in Retirement." https://pressroom.vanguard.com/nonindexed/Research-Planning-for-healthcare-costs-in-retirement_061918.pdf

care or recovery care costs. The Vanguard report referenced before only includes costs for medical, dental, and vision costs. We will look at the costs of long-term care and recovery care planning later in this section. For now, let's discuss how best to plan for the costs outlined by the report referenced above.

In 1981, I wrote my very first Medicare supplement plan. At that time, Medicare had two parts: A and B. Part A primarily covered hospital and skilled nursing care. Part B covered outpatient and physician charges. Times were pretty simple then. For most retirees, going on Medicare meant purchasing a Medicare Supplemental plan and they were all set on Part A, as most plans paid the deductibles and copay amounts in full. But finding the right plan to cover Part B benefits was more challenging. At that time, a retiree could be balance-billed whatever amount the doctor chose to bill. Medicare only paid 80 percent of an approved amount. For this reason, the company I was working with was one of the first to offer coverage for 100 percent of balance billing. By 1990, the number of doctors who had agreed to accept "assignment" (what Medicare approved) had grown substantially and even those physicians who chose not to accept assignment were now limited on what they could charge. The effect of this new legislation greatly reduced the impact of physician and outpatient charges to retirees, but they still faced unlimited out-of-pocket maximums.

In 1983, new rules begin to affect Part A of Medicare. Medicare began using what would become known as the DRG prospective payment system for hospital charges. Prior to this, hospitals billed Medicare for actual charges incurred once the patient was dismissed. For the retiree, the cost was only the initial deductible or daily co-payments if their stay ran past sixty days in a benefit period. Hospitals were free to pass on to Medicare the full cost of whatever the doctor had approved. With the passage of the new process, hospitals would now be paid a fixed dollar amount that was tied to the actual admitting diagnosis. The fixed dollar cost was based upon the average costs for treating a specific condition. The result caused many retirees to be dismissed earlier than they had been in previous years and coined the term "Quicker and Sicker," which began creating a new risk as more and more people were moved from the hospital to nursing homes.

Today, Medicare has four parts: A, B, C, and D. Parts A and B are considered part of original Medicare and retirees still have an unlimited exposure and thus most purchase one of the standardized Medicare Supplemental plans designed to help pay what original Medicare does not. These original Medicare recipients may choose to purchase a Part D plan (which provides prescription drug benefits) from a private carrier approved to offer Part D coverage in their area. Part C, also known as Medicare Advantage, is composed of the elements of A, B, and D (usually all rolled into one plan). These plans are underwritten by private insurance companies approved by Medicare. It is essential to seek out a professional who understands the various rules and enrollment periods available with all these differing ways to have Medicare benefits.

For most of my clients, original Medicare, a Medicare supplement, and a Part D plan is what I recommend (provided they can afford this approach), as it allows them to better budget for their medical costs. If the payment of premiums for this approach is not within reach, considering a Medicare Advantage plan that includes prescription drug benefits may be the solution. Please be careful in choosing one of these plans. It is essential that you understand the specific requirements to receive benefits for the plan you choose. Most Medicare Advantage plans require the use of a network or may require additional payments if you choose to use a provider out of network.

The larger issue for most retirees is how to cover the costs of long-term or recovery care. As noted in the charts above, this type of care can cost over $85,000 per person per year at current rates.

The decision on how to pay the costs of long-term care is a personal one. It comes down to three choices: Be rich, be poor, or be insured. This might sound brutal but remember that the risk of a retiree needing care is either 0 percent or 100 percent. You either need it or not. What if your risk is at 100 percent? [33]

At one time, there were several companies who offered long-term care insurance plans, and many were exceptional. Today there are only a few companies who still offer traditional coverage for long-term care. Many retirees are finding that what may be a better approach is to fund long-term care costs from cash flow (provided they have enough assets) or by moving a specified amount to one of the many hybrid long-term care and life plans now available. This approach has seen tremendous growth in recent years and is an option I usually explore with my clients. The hybrid approach guarantees the beneficiary or the beneficiary's family will receive a benefit, either as a payment for care, or a future death benefit.

Nothing in life is more personal than one's healthcare and as a cornerstone of the New Retirement Blueprint planning process, to neglect this area could lead to devastating results. As I stated earlier, the time to begin planning for health care is when you and your advisor work to prepare a written income plan. Income planning is truly the cornerstone of retirement and healthcare must be planned for in the process. Planning should begin as early as possible, as health becomes an issue if you choose an insured solution. If you don't have a written plan that includes a health care solution, you still should seek out an advisor who will provide you with a comprehensive plan that will address all five areas covered in this book. You can learn more at www.sokyadvisors.com.

---

[33] Jesse Slome. American Association for Long-Term Care Insurance. 2018. "What is the Probability You'll Need Long-Term Care? Is Long-Term Care Insurance a Smart Financial Move?" http://www.aaltci.org/long-term-care-insurance/learning-center/probability-long-term-care.php

Part Four: Action List

1. Health care planning is part of the income planning process. Don't do one without the other. Begin exploring your Medicare options no later than age sixty-four.
2. Learn which Medicare path is best for you and seek out the help of a licensed and certified advisor to choose your plan. To schedule a meeting with a certified advisor in the Medicare market, go to www.sokyadvisors.com.
3. Begin long-term planning as soon as possible. Health is a consideration.
4. Discuss with your family what care they may be willing or able to provide. Consider a hybrid policy versus a traditional long-term care plan. Seek out competent professional help.

PART FIVE

Legacy Planning

"A good man leaves an inheritance for his children's children"

-Solomon

The concept of leaving a legacy to those we leave behind is an ancient tradition. In the Bible, we see what is referred to as the passing of "the blessing" to the oldest son. This was the tradition of many cultures for centuries. This process was a way of controlling the future from the grave and was believed to be a sacred act that could not be broken. In the story of Jacob and Esau (Genesis Chapter 27), we see such an example. Jacob stole the blessing of Esau through deception of his aged father. Esau pleaded with his father to bless him as well, but there was no undoing what had been done.

The oldest known last will and testament was discovered in 1890 by a famous English archaeologist named William Flinders Petrie.[34] The document was found among the Egyptian pyramids.

---

[34] Lane V. Erickson. Racine Olson Law. December 4, 2018. "What We Can Learn from the Oldest Known Last Will and Testament."
https://www.racinelaw.net/blog/what-we-can-learn-from-the-oldest-known-last-will-and-testament/.

> *This document was written on a parchment/papyrus paper-like substance and was originally dated to have been created 2500 BC. It was later determined that this will was created in 1797 BC and refers to the creator of the will, whose name is Ankr-ren. It is also interesting to note that there were two witnesses to this will.*
>
> *Ankr-ren described himself to be a devoted servant of the superintendent of works where the pyramids were built. In his will, Ankr-ren gives all of his property to his brother, Uah, with instructions that forbid Uah from demolishing any of the houses given through his will. So, almost 4,000 years ago, we find ancient Egyptians using a document that is eerily similar to what we use today, including the signature of two witnesses.*

So, what compels humans to seek to leave a legacy? Besides the obvious examples of a parent providing for small children or a spouse providing for the one left behind, there are many other reasons.

I am a student of history, particularly interested in the founding fathers of our country. One of my favorite quotes from John Adams was, "I must study politics and war that my sons may have liberty to study mathematics and philosophy."[35] This was a form of leaving a legacy for his children. John knew, to gain the independence of a new country, he would have to build a political foundation and fight a war of independence that would allow his children the freedom to pursue the study of other math and sciences and provide the foundation upon which his grandchildren could then study art and philosophy. Most people I meet in this country strongly desire to make life easier for their children than what they experienced, much like John Adams. Some would say that we have made it too easy for our children and thus they have become spoiled and dependent. I can't argue that point, but I don't believe it is the passing of our wealth that creates this in our children, but

---

[35] John Adams. Shmoop. 1780. "1780 Letter."
https://www.shmoop.com/quotes/study-politics-war-sons-have-liberty.html

perhaps an emphasis on the passing of wealth over the passing of our core values about money.

Perhaps the great thing about creating the proper legal structures and taking the time to consider our mortality is not that we will pass our estate on in an efficient manner, but that we can use this process to possibly protect our heirs from themselves and create much more than a legacy of money. It provides us an opportunity to continue to instruct our loved ones from the great beyond.

When you consider that one out of every six retired Americans is a millionaire,[36] then most of us have good reason to want to consider our options for legacy planning. The baby boom generation will retire with more wealth than any group in history. Average wealth for American retirees is $752,000, which has more than doubled since 1989, according to the United Income report referenced below. However, according to AARP, 42 percent of boomers don't have any kind of essential estate planning documents.[37] In Part Five of this book, we will address many of the concerns of retirees when it comes to legacy planning and share some ideas on how to prepare if you haven't already taken actions.

Although there are some similar concepts and tools involved, legacy planning is a bit more complex than estate planning. A legacy is something that will hopefully last longer, something that can set the foundation for second and even third generations down the line.

The very first thing you need to know about legacy planning is that you don't want to do it alone. A competent and trusted attorney will save you much more than the costs. My first experience

---

[36] Matt Fellowes, Lincoln Plews. United Income. "The State of Retirees." https://unitedincome.com/documents/papers/UnitedIncomeStateOfRetirees.pdf.
[37] Barbranda Lumpkins Walls. AARP. February 24, 2017. "Haven't Done a Will Yet?" https://www.aarp.org/money/investing/info-2017/half-of-adults-do-not-have-wills.html

with attorneys was that I had no experience! I entered into a business partnership in 1995 with only a handshake and no legal counsel. Four years later, I found that my "exit strategy" was not as I understood it to be. Thankfully, I had a good partner who was very fair when we parted. My second experience with attorneys was when I sought their advice but did not follow it. It cost me thousands of dollars. My experience today is to seek good counsel and listen to what they tell you to do. Wealthy people understand this and secure their wealth with the proper documents and legal structures to pass wealth down to the next generation or their favorite charities.

Legacy planning does not have to be overly expensive. According to a recent article,

"If your current family and financial situations do not warrant the need for a revocable living trust, then your foundational estate plan will include the following four important legal documents:

1. Last Will and Testament
2. Advance Medical Directive
3. Living Will
4. Financial Power of Attorney"[38]

There is absolutely no reason that every person reading this book should not have these minimal documents. I have a membership with a company called Legal Shield, and for only $26 per month, I receive many forms of legal benefits and can have these four documents created and amended or redone every two years by a licensed attorney.

For those who need a more sophisticated plan because of accumulated wealth and/or business interests, a different kind of will, called a pour-over will, would be advised. this legacy plan should

---

[38] Julie Garber. The Balance. February 22, 2019. "Essential Estate Planning Documents. https://www.thebalance.com/what-are-the-essential-estate-planning-documents-3505184.

also include a revocable living trust, advance medical directive, living will, and financial power of attorney. These documents round out a more sophisticated legacy plan.

Let's look at each of these products and why they are important.

- A last will and testament is generally found in an estate plan, rather than a legacy plan. It's the main document that details how your property is to be distributed after your death. If you have children under the age of eighteen, you would use this document to appoint a legal guardian for your children.
- When an individual has a revocable living trust, the trust documents become the guiding document for one's asset. The accompanying will in this legacy plan would be called a pour-over will; it will address only those assets that were not transferred to the trust before your death, not your entire estate and assets.
- With a revocable living trust, you will draw up documents and provide instructions that address financial issues and decisions related to your assets while you are alive and once you have died. For example, it should address the scenario of handling your wealth if you are mentally incapacitated, guaranteeing that your wishes are carried out as you want.
- An advance medical directive declares a person who will relate your wishes and who will be the decisionmaker for addressing your health care needs in case you are unable to make those decisions yourself. It should address medical decision-making not only if you are physically unable to make decisions, but also if you are mentally unable to make decisions.
- A living will is also related to your medical care that deals more specifically with health issues that are terminal, life-

threatening, or end-of-life. This is where you let your loved ones know your wishes on life-sustaining procedures.

- A financial power of attorney names a person(s) you want to manage or handle what are called titled financial assets, such as banking accounts, retirement plans, or other such products in your name. A *durable* financial power of attorney becomes effective as soon as you sign it, while the *springing* power of attorney "springs" into action if you become mentally incapacitated.

As you can see, the degree of planning required will differ greatly from one person to the next, but every retiree should make certain they have the essential legal documents in place at a minimum.

Many times, I talk with clients who are concerned about losing their legacy to the cost of long-term health care. While we covered the three ways to plan for this in Part Four, we did not elaborate on one of the three choices. The three choices are be rich, be poor, or be insured. We discussed the insured solutions in Part Four of this book. In the next few pages we are going to discuss being poor. In the United States, over 4 million people are covered by the joint federal-and-state program called Medicaid. This program will pay the costs of long-term care, provided you have met all the requirements. The bottom line for qualification is that you must be too "poor" to pay for your own care. Obviously, if you do not have enough assets to pay the cost, then you will qualify, but there are legal remedies available that can allow you to be "poor" but still have enough income until care is needed.

Let me very clear that this type of planning should only be done with an attorney who specializes in the process and said process varies wildly from state to state.

As I mentioned earlier, the approach used by many large endowments is a foundational component of the New Retirement Blueprint approach. Endowments look for the long haul and realize that the wealth they manage if properly protected can serve the needs of many future generations. A lot can be learned from institutions that have been using funds provided decades ago to continue to provide educational resources today to students who weren't even born when the donations were received. A good friend and mentor of mine who also wrote the forward for this book says, "success leaves clues". So, follow the example of these large endowments and don't leave legacy planning to chance.

Part Five: Action List

1. Start today. Make that call.
2. Seek professional legal counsel. This is NOT a do-it-yourself piece of the financial puzzle.
3. Consider your spouse and what they will have to live on when you're gone. Make sure your income plan is sufficient to provide for them when you are gone. Most surviving spouses will lose anywhere from 25 to 50 percent of monthly income when their partner dies.
4. Remember, legacy planning is about more than money.
5. If your current advisor is only showing you how to invest, consider a new advisor.

Conclusion

There are many ways to provide a financial legacy for your family. In our modern society, one can provide a significant financial sum for a minimal amount of money spent each month on life insurance. Given time and a free-enterprise economy, saving even modest sums consistently can grow a sizeable inheritance, as has been the case for millions of Americans in their 401(k) plans. I work with people of varying degrees of financial net worth, but the common denominator for all of us is that 100 percent of us will eventually need a legacy plan in place. Don't put off today what your family may regret tomorrow. Procrastination does not benefit you or your family.

I want to end with a quick story from my own life. A few days ago, as I write this, I buried my mother. She was only seventeen years older than me, and we always said we had to raise one another. She reminded me a week before she passed away that I had promised her many years ago I would speak at her funeral. I assured her as she lay in the hospital bed that I would keep my promise. As I spent some time the day before her funeral preparing what I was about to say, I considered the legacy that my seventy-four-year-old mother had passed down to me and my sister. While I did not expect to receive anything financial, she had spent seventy-four years defining who she was and shaping who we had become.

My mom was a very intelligent woman who went back to college twenty-five years after dropping out of high school and graduated with honors. She walked with confidence and took great pride in always being the best at whatever job she was doing. She was a strong, independent woman who never doubted her worth or her capability. In every job she ever had, she was promoted to a position with more responsibility.

While Mom was not a wealthy woman, she left an incredible legacy. Growing up as number seven of eight children in a sharecropper family, money was scarce, but love and values were strong. When she left home at the age of fifteen to marry my father, she immediately went to work, and she continued to do so until her health kept her from it. My mother left me and my sister with many blessings that cannot be enumerated. She passed down her confidence and her work ethic. She passed down a love for life and a desire to always be the best at whatever you did. I am thankful for this legacy, and I am fully persuaded that if I can pass on to my five children the lessons of life that my mom passed to me, they can have as much success as they desire.

Please, don't put your planning off. As a financial advisor, I can assist you in many ways as you create your plan for living, but only you can take the action required to plan your legacy.

Acknowledgments

I have said for the past twenty years that I was going to write this book. It would not have happened without the support and input of several people whom I want to acknowledge. My wife, Glenda, who has encouraged and pushed me to set aside the time necessary to make this happen. The many clients who took the time to proof the manuscript and provide feedback and for allowing me to be their financial guide. My children, who have always been the motivation for why I do what I do because I want their futures to be as bright as possible and for them to know and understand sound financial principles. I would not be in this business had my cousin, Barbara Costellow, not led the way for me to follow. Lastly, I want to thank my father for never doubting my ability to accomplish any goal I have ever set.

About the Author

ALLEN COSTELLOW, RFC®, CTS®
President & CEO

Allen is focused on helping clients work toward their retirement dreams through a well-thought-out financial strategy for retirement.

After growing up in a middle-class, blue-collar home where finances were always a struggle, Allen joined the financial industry, becoming an insurance agent in 1979.

In 2006, Allen launched his own financial services firm to help retirees and their families develop a financial strategy that works to build and preserve their lifestyle. He truly enjoys helping people to maximize their income—and minimize taxation—in retirement.

Since entering the financial services in 1979, Allen has personally worked with over 2,000 clients in the south-central Kentucky region. Today, many of Allen's new clients are children whose parents he worked with years ago.

As the president and founder of Southern Kentucky Advisors, Allen has surrounded himself with a team of people committed to bringing increasing value to the lifetime clients of the firm.

Allen has passed the Series 7, 63 and 65 securities exams and holds licenses in life, health, property, casualty, Medicare and long-term care insurance in multiple states. He is registered as an Investment Advisor Representative and has earned his Registered Financial Consultant (RFC) and Certified Tax Specialist (CTS) designations. His professional memberships include the National Association of Insurance and Financial Advisors (NAIFA) and the International Association of Registered Financial Consultants (IARFC). Allen also has been featured on "MomsEveryday" on WBKO-TV as well as "VIP Bowling Green."

Allen is an active member in his local church and has served on several advisory boards of companies and nonprofits.

He resides in Bowling Green, Kentucky, with his wife, Glenda. They have five children and seven grandchildren. Allen and his family spend quality time year-round and especially enjoy two family trips to the beach and the mountains.

Contact Us

I hope this book has helped you gain in confidence and feel better-prepared for the road that lies ahead. If what I have discussed resonates with you, or if you're ready to go over your own financial situation, contact my office. We'd be happy to help you or refer you to someone who can.

Allen Costellow
Southern Kentucky Advisors
https://sokyadvisors.com
Phone: 270.904.7624 | Fax: 270.640.0885
admin@sokyadvisors.com

730 Fairview Ave., Suite B5
Bowling Green, KY 42101

www.ingramcontent.com/pod-product-compliance
Lightning Source LLC
Chambersburg PA
CBHW070805220526
45466CB00002B/551